Staffroom Secrets

A teacher's guide to your child's primary education

Jane Chappell

Copyright © 2020 Jane Chappell
All rights reserved.
ISBN: 978-1-8380095-0-2

DEDICATION

Beth, Lottie and Flo – my favourite teachers

Nanny Mum – my Wendy Moira Angela Darling

John – my undercover superhero

Please be aware that when I speak of *parents*, I include all those who take on parental responsibilities: grandparents, carers, foster parents, aunts and uncles, guardians, etc. Having worked with exceptional carers, I wanted readers to be assured that, as I wrote, these *parents* were very much in my thoughts.

CONTENTS

Introduction

1. It's all about you — 1
2. Nowhere to run to, nowhere to hide — 12
3. Head, shoulders, knees and toes — 16
4. I heard it through the grapevine — 31
5. Video killed the radio star — 42
6. This is how we do it — 51
7. What a wonderful world this would be — 63
8. A,B,C easy as 1,2,3 — 70
9. Ironic — 76
10. Knock three times — 89
11. Do re me fa so la ti do — 113
12. Stop, look, listen to your heart — 117
13. It ain't over till it's over — 123

A handy guide — 133

INTRODUCTION

When I set about writing *Staffroom Secrets*, I was clear I wanted it to be for all parents, just as my classroom is for all children. This book is for anyone who wants to help their children have a happy, healthy schooling experience. This book is for twenty-two-year-old me, who had aspirations for her daughter but nowhere to go for solid, comprehensive advice; it's for my cousin, whose son recently started school; it's for the mums I overheard on a train to London, who spoke about nothing but how baffled they were by their children's maths homework. Whether you have a PhD or a handful of GCSEs, *Staffroom Secrets* has been written for you. I wrote it because I trained as a primary school teacher after I'd had three children, and I spent a lot of time saying, "I wish I'd known that!" I felt compelled to reveal all I had discovered with parents, who I knew (like me) wanted the best for their children. I put pen to paper with aspirations of creating a little book I could gift to my children when they are grown and have children of their own…

This is for parents whose children go to state schools, faith schools, independent schools, boarding schools, rural schools and inner-city schools. Finally, this is for primary school teachers – my friends and colleagues. May it go some way towards bridging the gap between the kitchen table and the school desk, and create a clearer path of communication between parent, teacher and child.

ACKNOWLEDGEMENTS

Every child I have taught has made this book possible. In particular, I would like to acknowledge the staff, children and families from Culverstone Green Primary School in Kent for affording me the opportunity to teach from my heart and create change.

IT'S ALL ABOUT YOU

Parents are the first and most enduring
educators of their children[*]

My mum always made it clear that she believed in me. "You're being raised to change the world, not beds!" I may have been the goofy girl with NHS glasses, a gingham school dress from Woolies (despite my school having a no uniform policy) and free school meals, but I was raised to think big. We lived in a horrible council flat in a 'colourful' part of Medway, but my mum always had pride, even if she didn't have hot water. We were over-crowded (I shared a room with Mum and Dad), but Mum made space for opportunities in my life – she took me to clubs and talked to me like I was the adult she wanted me to be. We had our daily challenges: Dad was poorly with manic depression, which is what bipolar was called then, and paranoid schizophrenia, but somehow mum managed to raise us with optimistic eyes, thankful hearts and the capacity to dream.

---

[*] QCA Early Learning Goals, page 17

READ WITH YOUR CHILD

She was always reading stories. I have three brothers: Andy, a firefighter; Brian, a whiz-kid engineer with a first-class degree (can you be a whiz-kid in your fifties?); and Adrian, a CEO with a CBE. As Dumbledore says, "It matters not what someone is born, but what they grow to be."[*] Our mum created opportunities for us; she read books and fuelled dreams. If this book had been around when we were little, she'd have jumped on it (she'd actually have caught the bus to the library and filled in a request slip) because it represents an opportunity. My wish for this little book is that it creates opportunities by cultivating a fairer, healthier playing field in our classrooms. I suppose it's been written in homage to my mum, who raised me to believe that regardless of who you are or where you come from, you should try to change the world and make it a better place. She was preaching that long before Shakira had heard of Disney's *Zootopia*, but we like what they've done with it..!

My mum is a huge motivating force behind what I have set out to do here… Her unshakeable belief in her children's potential and her steadfast, quiet determination to support us, whilst we reached for our once distance dreams, is beyond commendable – especially when you consider the backdrop to our adventures. Mum had to endure more than her fair share of twists and turns in our journey, but she persisted. I am confident *Staffroom Secrets* would have served her well. It would have been a channel for her extraordinary energy, and it would have saved her from enduring so many frustrations and setbacks. This book explores two key areas: navigating our primary school system and optimising the

---

[*] Harry Potter and the Goblet of Fire

exceptional drive parents have to support their children. By using the book to avoid unnecessary emotional twists and turns and costly setbacks, you and your child will be able to get the most from the primary school years and have fun in the process. As a teacher, I believe it is part of my job to give parents tools to help them support their children. I hope *Staffroom Secrets* will become your 'go-to' guide when you find yourself looking for some trustworthy advice or practical ideas to support your child in school.

Like every teacher I know, I have studied hard, worked ridiculously long hours, and lost sleep over children in my care; I can say, hand on heart, that I have slogged to be the best teacher I can be. I have cried with pride, sobbed with upset, caught more coughs, colds and bugs than anyone should have to tolerate, but I know I will never be the most influential teacher in any child's life. I fervently believe the teacher who has the most impact on a child will never be found in a classroom – that's because it's the person (or people) who raise them and endeavour to be there, throughout their childhood. It's probably you – the one who has grabbed this book and is about to start turning the pages. You are the most important teacher in your child's life. I'd like to take this opportunity to formally welcome you to the profession. Be warned my friend, the pay is rubbish but, to be fair, the rewards: bountiful.

If a little one in your life is about to start 'Big School' then you may well be wondering what you can do to ease their transition into the world of formal education – a place in which they will be spending the majority of their formative years. Or perhaps you are part way through the process and want to re-focus your attention. Whether you are reading this with your first child in mind or your twelfth great-grandchild, welcome. This little book is for you. I hope that it, and of course your conscience, will be your guide through the primary years. I liken this book to a trip to the opticians: it's an opportunity to re-focus and see the world of education through a slightly different lens. Take from it all you can **except** this: guilt! Don't reflect on things you've done in the past and give yourself a hard time. I've done so many things that I wouldn't dream of doing now. My mum says the same… The joy of a misguided choice is the learning we take from it as we continue to journey forwards. I'm not going to put myself on a destructive guilt-trip over things 'Jane-of-the-past' got up to. I need to thank her for her endeavours in bringing me here today. Be kind to yourself and, whilst you're at it, congratulate yourself for popping into the 'Opticians for Proactive Parents!' If you struggled at school, if you feel like the 'system' failed you and you are worried about how well placed you are to guide your child, I want to reassure you: I muddled through my GCSEs, my husband turned up (to most of his) but left with even less than I did. Neither of us did A levels, and he (as yet) has no degree. I came to further and higher education much later in life – after my eldest had sat her GCSEs, which (proud parent alert) she smashed! I was so determined that she'd do well. I was obsessed! Not always in a healthy way, I'll admit (that's those misguided choices), but I was engaged, active and open to learn. That's what mattered. *My* academic prowess: inconsequential, *my* history: just that – history, *my* grades: irrelevant. This was about *her* and what I could do to make good stuff happen in her life, and, from what I figured, doing well at school was a good place to start. Experience has taught me that this model cuts both ways: parents with glittering academic careers are capable of hampering their own children's academic potential, when they fail to recognise what their children need in order to succeed in a healthy way.

Where to begin? How do we best help our children? I believe we need to mobilise an army of enthusiastic, positive parents with a very clear message:

> The curriculum is challenging – your child needs YOU
>
> STAFFROOM SECRET

Consider this guide as a bit of a heads up; this is your map to navigate beyond colouring-in and 'Show and Tell'. Do not, for one misguided second, think I am implying our teachers are failing our children, and so you need to step up and take over! Nothing could be further from the truth. I am proud to be counted amongst some of the most dedicated, highly trained professional teachers in the world. But we must face facts: targets are high (some say to make us globally competitive), and so culturally we need to adjust. Most of us would agree that fear, cramming, family shame, longer school days and shorter holidays are not the way to achieve aspirational targets. In my experience, there are creative, enjoyable, simple solutions to explore in the pursuit of primary goals, as well as good old-fashioned values to deploy, such as perseverance and practice. The key to it all, however, is a positive partnership between school, children and home.

Some of my dearest friends argue that it's not their job to teach their children, but there are countless studies to argue that disassociating from your child's education puts them at a huge disadvantage. Put frankly, if you do not support your child's learning at home, don't expect them to reach their full potential in the classroom. That doesn't mean all parents should rush to night-school and become qualified teachers – it just means you need to take a healthy interest in your child's learning journey and make supporting what's going on in the classroom a part of everyday life, at home. Of course, lots of parents already support learning at home, but the problem is (excuse the school report pun) they 'could do better'! That's not a criticism – it's a well-meaning rallying cry. I'm not suggesting that in the main effort isn't being spent or passion is lacking.

In the primary years, children develop their metacognition: they learn how to learn. By building strong metacognition in the primary years, children have a better chance of becoming confident, independent learners in their secondary years. I want us to work on that; I want us to give our children the tools they need to enjoy learning. We need to build good habits into their daily lives (and ours) in order to best support them. Be under no illusion, this is a serious challenge, but the sooner you start, the better. As teachers and parents, we need to elevate learning to be as engaging and exciting as playing on the iPad. We need to create a 'buzz' in their brains from solving a maths problem or talking about a book they've read. We are in competition with the fast-paced, modern world and all its corporate funding. Children are used to instant gratification and being 'fed' information. We need to get them into the habit of creating their own exciting content and exploring that. We need to be engaging, authentic, exciting and present. My job description says 'teacher' but I reckon 'high-end children's entertainer' is more appropriate. I know that creating a 'buzz' engages their brains, and they learn more effectively as a result. It's that simple.

The burden of teaching our children cannot fall solely on the shoulders of those in the classroom – many teachers are at breaking point, trying to get all the children in their care to the 'expected standard' as set out by the government. The government's expectation of what our children can achieve shifted dramatically in 2014. The challenging curriculum is part of the reason the profession has been in crisis, why many teachers are leaving the job they loved, and why many are suffering with stress and anxiety. However, it's the system we live in; it's our children's reality, and, all the time it exists as such, it is our duty, as parents and teachers alike, to support them as best we can. Trust me, I am not waving a flag in support of the system in which I work – if I were waving anything, it would be a wand. In my experience, very few parents realise the extent of change to the curriculum and the implications of the change to their role at home. Those who are aware of the implications are usually uncertain of how to best support their children or tackle unfamiliar challenges. That's why we need to communicate more effectively, teacher to parent and back again. This book is as much for our teachers' benefit as it is for the parents – if parents better understand the challenges involved in educating their children, and they are given the skills and tools to support them effectively, the teachers in the classroom will, in turn, be better supported to do an even better job. Win, win, win. As my little Flo says, 'Teamwork makes the dream work, mummy!'

I think of our classroom teachers as superheroes: they regularly save the day without so much as a Batmobile or web-flicking wrist; they count themselves lucky if they have enough pencils to go around and a glue-stick between two. They regularly deal with a multitude of dangerous substances leaking from all sorts of places, from unpredictable little creatures, without flinching or heaving. Granted, their costumes are more Clark Kent than Superman, but there's a reason for that: the trend for wearing your pants on the outside of your trousers is bad enough in reception classes, and they don't want to set a precedent! Sure, they all have their Kryptonite (decaf coffee, wet break, the Christmas play…) but they soldier on. Our teachers are under-resourced, underpaid, undercover (pants on the inside) superheroes!

> Teachers are not perfect, they have flaws just like all the other superheroes, but they are superheroes, nevertheless. I therefore declare (in this little book), they shall be known as such!

STAFFROOM SECRET

As the demands on our children are significant and often overwhelming, they need support at home – like never before – if we are to best protect them from the mounting pressure they face. As adults, we need to be acutely aware of a modern-day phenomenon: alarming numbers of children are suffering from depression and anxiety, with cases escalating at a startling rate. I was listening to the radio in the car today, and the detrimental impact on children's mental health associated with raising educational standards was part of the discussion[*]. My recent Youth Mental Health First Aid training highlighted just how serious the problem is. The following statistics have all been taken from my handbook, and I found them to be sad but not surprising as they correlate with all the anecdotal evidence I have encountered.

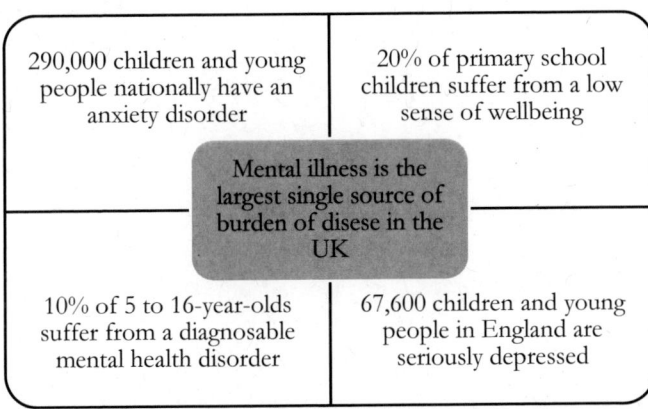

The catalyst behind these statistics is complex, and I am not suggesting our education system is entirely to blame, but I do sincerely believe it is significantly contributing to the mess we find ourselves in. So what next? We know there is a problem. How do we go about fixing it? Well, I am optimistic because I work with children and their

---

[*] Jeremy Vine BBC Radio 2 (06.06.19) Nick Harrop, Young minds

optimism has rubbed off on me. I believe we have the power to create change in our homes – substantial change that will support our children. I maintain that the majority of our children are capable of meeting the high standards expected of them without it causing anxiety, depression and low self-esteem. Moreover, I believe they can meet their 'age related expectation' by making learning what it should be: child's play! We (parents and teachers) need to approach the problem from a different angle and adjust the lenses in our metaphorical specs. The extra-special, good news is that parents can do it straight away. You don't have to wait for approval from the SLT (senior leadership team), a mandate from government, a new Ofsted framework or a curriculum overhaul to be signed off by the governors! You can start today. That is exciting. Let's be excited, not angry – it's so much more productive.

The vast majority of parents want to do all they can to support their children. They often ask for advice at parent consultations, and I rapidly try to fire off as much information as I can. The problem is, there's never enough time. I prided myself on parental involvement in the classroom, but I never felt like I was doing enough. It was impossible of course. I had 32 children who needed me to plan their lessons, teach them and give them feedback on their lovely work. I had NHS forms to fill in, files to keep, records to update, displays to conjure, test papers to mark, data to compile, staff meetings, courses to attend, parent consultations, pupil premium meetings, curriculum development afternoons, online training, Music and RE to co-ordinate, plays to put on, working-walls to design, class trips to plan that required risk assessments, the PTA to meet with, reports to write, governors to meet with, etc. That's why *Staffroom Secrets* was born. I was chatting with the glorious Tracey Wakefield, our class TA (teaching assistant), about all the things parents could do to best support their children in the classroom, when I joked that *You'd need to write a book!*

So here it is. Composed with full permission granted from my long-suffering children – the ones at home, not the ones in the classroom: Beth, Lottie and Flo. They've graciously allowed me to expose all our shortcomings (well, mine, at their expense) and our triumphs, which they are claiming as their own. Throughout, I'll gift you with my own embarrassing mistakes (you're welcome), my advice as a teacher (hush, hush – staffroom secrets), and the top-tips gathered from my superhero friends and colleagues. Positive pants on people, coats on heads, but don't you dare put your arms through the sleeves; we're going through the school gates, and we're going to fly!

p.s. I've just read the first chapter to my three girls, to see if they think the tone is okay. The eldest two were full of encouragement but Flo looked concerned and warned, "You should let them know the 'flying' bit at the end is metaphorical, or they'll think you're actually going to teach them to fly, and everyone will be really disappointed!" Honestly, everyone's a critic...*

---

* Metaphorical is in the vocabulary list at the back of the book. My 9-year-old used that word because I've taught her how to. She's not 'bright', 'talented' or 'brainy'. If anything, she's struggling with speech that is not literal; it confuses her when people don't say what they actually mean. Children benefit from knowing what metaphorical means because they'll be expected to know about it before they leave primary school.

NOWHERE TO RUN TO, NOWHERE TO HIDE
All experts were once beginners

If I had a pound for every time I heard something along the lines of, *It's unbelievable what they have to know!* I'd be in the Bahamas with a garland around my neck, not in my kitchen with a scarf: it's freezing[*]. I believe the subtext of the surprise is often: *It's unbelievable what I don't know!* Too many adults are scared to reveal they don't know 'stuff', and fear can bring out the worst in people. I've been directly confronted by adults who, through misplaced frustration, lash out at superheroes and their children when faced with inevitable primary school challenges. I've got my hands up here: guilty as charged. In the past, I've been embarrassed (correction: ashamed) that I've not known or understood stuff in the primary curriculum. I became a primary school teacher after having three children; before that, I ran theatre

---

[*] This is an example of hyperbole. It's not literally freezing. Hyperbole is a fancy term for exaggerating. If you didn't know about it, now you do. It's no big deal. It will help your child to know about hyperbole when they are at school.

workshops for schools. Not knowing things, back in the day, unleashed a powerful, primal fear in me. I thought I should know (I definitely thought I should understand at first glance) material aimed at those under twelve! I thought I must be unintelligent. Really pretty stupid. Obviously, I strived to keep that hidden – I didn't want to embarrass my children. Driven mainly by shame, I ventured (in secret) to an adult education class, where I had an epiphany. My coke drinking, richly tattooed, laid back dude of a tutor declared that he didn't get s*** half the time. This guy had a degree in maths. I thought he knew everything. Yet, here he was with a GCSE question that had him scratching his head. He was open, unashamed, curious and happy to put his head together with mine to puzzle it out. Boom! Game changer. He was like, *So what?* He didn't 'get' something. It was just some stuff. Since becoming a teacher, I have discovered the art of pretending you don't know. If that's what this chap was doing, it worked! I fell for it, and it was a huge moment in my life. On the whole, I believe my generation failed to benefit from superheroes who declared they didn't know… Not knowing, back then, was perceived as a weakness; superheroes were not weak. Superheroes were clever – their 'intelligence' was an integral part of their armour. They were knowledgeable disciplinarians who said stuff I had to remember. If I didn't remember it, I must be a bit stupid.

Those who support children must realise that it does not matter if you don't know stuff. We need to rid ourselves of shame. It's time to embrace *I don't know*, just be sure to add *but we can find out together*.

READ WITH YOUR CHILD

STAFFROOM SECRET

> **Remember:**
> In school, children are relentlessly faced with new ideas and concepts to master; they will learn from you (more than anyone) if that is an opportunity for fun exploration or a source of upset, angst and self-doubt.

Your children need to see you struggle and not understand. Moreover, they need to see you face challenges and problems with an upbeat curiosity. For your part, Coke and tattoos are optional.

It really doesn't matter if you have no idea what a prefix is, how to use the Singapore bar method or when King Henry VIII took an axe to poor old Anne. I wouldn't have a clue about Anne without looking it up, and I watched the Tudor Horrible Histories on stage last weekend – that doesn't make me stupid, it means I'm not great at remembering dates. I have to make up daft stories to retain them.* The point I am at pains to make is that regardless of whether you have a PhD or not so much as a GCSE, your child needs you. Indeed, a significant adult with no

---

* I just looked it up: 19th May 1536. My silly story: Anne is an exhausted schoolteacher. As she returns to the classroom from packing the children off, she looks up at the clock to see it's **15:36**. There are just **19** days left until the end of term; exhausted, she turns to the executioner and pleads, "**May** you just chop it off!" And he did!

qualifications who is involved in their child's education is far more effective than one with a PhD who is not.

Onwards and upwards. Let's ditch the fear and have some fun! As they said on the playground in 1983, *Don't be chicken!*

HEAD, SHOULDERS, KNEES AND TOES
Cranium, clavicle, patella, phalanges

Before we dive in, I wanted to share our National Curriculum Key Stages, so you have an idea of how a school is structured.

Early Years

Age 3 - 4
Nursery
Early Years Foundation Stage 1

Age 4 - 5
Reception
Early Years Foundation Stage 2

Key Stage 1

Age 5 - 6
Year 1
Key Stage 1

Age 6 - 7
Year 2
Key Stage 1

Key Stage 2

Age 7 - 8
Year 3
Age 8 - 9
Year 4
Lower Key Stage 2

Age 9 - 10
Year 5
Age 10 - 11
Year 6
Upper Key Stage 2

Ask any reception class superhero what they wish children knew before they joined their class, and I guarantee A,B,C and 1,2,3 will be near the bottom of their list, if indeed it features at all. So many of us, myself included, are eager to give our children a head-start in life, and so, with misguided urgency, we fall foul of prioritising all the wrong goals. Some twenty-odd years ago, I remember 'cramming' Annie Apple, Bouncy Ben and Curious Cat with Beth like her life depended on it. The title of this chapter is no joke. I'm embarrassed to admit I taught Beth cranium, clavicle, patella, phalanges (and most of the other bones in her body) before she started school. She loved it – I thought I was doing a stellar job! Her superhero would have been happier had I poured my energies into ensuring she could zip up her coat, change her shoes in a timely manner and blow her nose more discretely! A classroom of 30 four-year-olds who can recite the alphabet is all very well and good, but if none of them can go to the loo independently, get their coats on or change for PE without help, valuable learning time is inevitably lost.

Independence is so important – it gives a child self-esteem and is the foundation on which superheroes can build. To become independent you must, of course, be resilient because those skills – getting dressed, folding clothes, tidying up – are often hard-won and require resilience to be successfully mastered. Ask any superhero to name a nemesis and you can be sure that 'learned-helplessness' is one you'll hear again and again. Here is where I stand (as a mum), guilty as charged. I've been there – rushing, stressed, frustrated or well-meaning, loving, underestimating… *I'll do the shoes/ You've done the buttons all wonky/ We haven't got time, just let mummy help you/ You might hurt yourself so let me.* With my youngest, in particular, I've had that urge to keep her young – knowing I won't be having any more. To compound matters, she has had no reason to 'step up', take on responsibility or help like her sisters had to. It's common – we see it in school a lot. It often (not always – don't write to me!) affects only-children and youngest siblings.

> "Never help a child with a task at which he feels he can succeed."
>
> Maria Montessori

STAFFROOM SECRET

I have to be strict with myself and as self-aware as possible. I have a responsibility to ensure my child is not 'that' child in the classroom – the one who stands there helplessly, assuming an adult will come and fix every problem that arises. I struggle at times. Parenting is a struggle. However, I firmly believe we have a duty as parents to enable our children for the classroom, and that means it's our job to teach the basics – not the superheroes'. Be strict with yourself and encourage your child's independence. So what if their attempt at something isn't perfect? It's not supposed to be – they're learning something new. Can you remember how it feels to learn something? If you can't, I strongly suggest you try something as quickly as possible: sign-language, the recorder, crocheting, anything. It will undoubtedly heighten the empathy you have with your child when they struggle with supposedly 'simple' tasks. In learning something new, you will become a better teacher.

I asked Charlotte Wakefield, my friend and EYFS (Early Years Foundation Stage) superhero, what her wish list would look like.

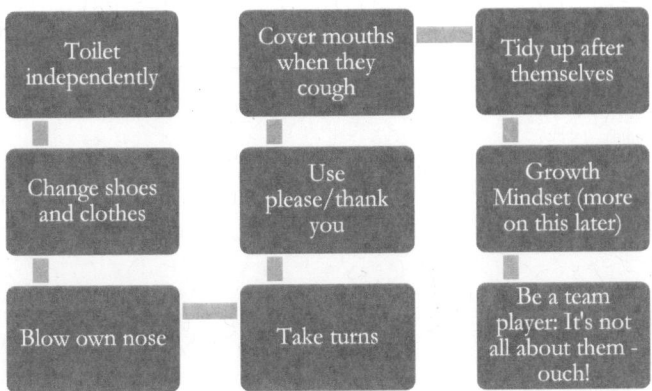

Toilet independently

In December 2018, Ofsted's chief inspector, Amanda Spielman, set out her concerns regarding the rising number of children starting school without being able to carry out basic functions like using the loo. She concluded:

> "This is difficult for teachers, disruptive for other children and has a terrible social impact on the children affected. This is wrong. Toilet training is the role of parents and carers and should not be left to schools. Only in the most extreme cases should parents be excused from this most basic of parenting tasks."
>
> Amanda Spielman

STAFFROOM SECRET

Successful toilet training takes time, extraordinary patience and sustained effort. If you need support, I'd suggest the NHS online guide is a good place to start. I can hear the echoes of superheroes up and down the land urging me to make it clear that successful toilet training is not simply about doing the 'do' in the right place and in time! It's about tidying up after yourself, flushing the loo and washing your hands – thoroughly. For obvious reasons, schools and germs can go hand-in-hand; make sure your child knows how to wash their hands properly, in a bid to minimise the spread of all those delightful childhood illnesses…

If your child is having difficulties using the loo, you should consult your doctor and let the school know. Please don't be embarrassed to talk to your child's superhero about toileting problems. It's our job to listen and, honestly, anyone I've ever worked with has taken toileting problems in their stride – it's part and parcel of the job. Keeping lines of communication open is key to the child's eventual, successful outcome. 'Bladder and Bowel UK' estimates that 28% of children and adolescents encounter toileting problems and need support. You are not alone.

To the Batmobile, Robin!

We know it takes oodles of practice and hefty dollops of patience, but superheroes need parents to train little sidekicks to move, fast! Robin would be no good to Batman if he were still struggling with his tights when the Batmobile was revved and ready to go…

Picture the scene: everyone's lined up and effervescent about using the apparatus in the hall. Bear in mind, the superhero has probably just spent their break time setting up the equipment, when what they really needed was some peace and quiet and a coffee. Then, consider that they've worked hard to design a lesson plan to meet all the necessary criteria: safe warm-up, familiarisation of equipment, health and safety considerations, clear demonstration, a balance between aerobic and anaerobic work stations, focus on balance and strength, the pairing of major muscle groups, developmental stretches, Amendeep's asthma, Sienna's verruca, Mildred's plasters for her earrings, differentiation etc., all masterfully woven into the theme of the term's topic – minibeasts! Most of the eager butterflies, worms and caterpillars are ready and wriggling by the door, but, unfortunately, a handful of children have their shorts on their heads and have managed to lose their t-shirts. Amanda Spielman's words start ringing in our superhero's ears: **"This is difficult for teachers, disruptive for other children and has a terrible social impact on the children affected. This is wrong."** Valuable time is lost, the lesson is compromised, the superhero ends up being the 'parent' and other children become disruptive or disengaged through frustration and disappointment. Make no mistake, four-year-olds will waste no time in blaming those they think responsible for holding up their fun. Everyone loses out. I reiterate at this point – I know these are not easy skills for children to master, but the vast majority can do it. If, after a sustained effort, your child cannot master these skills, you will need to see your GP for support and guidance.

Children are surprisingly capable when we allow them to be. My eyes were opened when my second child, Lottie, started at our local Montessori pre-school. The women who ran that place were not superheroes – they were goddesses. Their expectations of the children were so much higher than mine. They would very calmly show three-year-olds how to fold and hang clothes and then simply give them all the time they needed to master the skill. They would gently correct mistakes, they never sought perfection, they trusted the child's innate curiosity to keep them on task for a reasonable amount of time, and they never went overboard with unnecessary praise. Pay particular attention here – this is where the growth mindset features[*] (not that it was called 'growth mindset' back then). The superheroes did not want the children to expect or, worse still, need external praise to get a basic task done; self-satisfaction proved to be the only motivator they needed. It was such a calm environment. The school ran itself. I remember going there for the first time and seeing this adorable dot (not yet three-and-a-half) laying the table for his snack. Without a jot of adult intervention, he got a name label from a drawer and popped it on a table together with a placemat, plate and glass which he took from a shelf. He then walked to the fridge and took out his snack, set everything out on the table, carried a Pyrex jug of water to his glass and expertly filled it before replacing the jug. When the snack was finished, he tidied everything away. The goddess spoke once: to remind him to tuck in his chair; to ensure it didn't get in anyone's way. Mind blown! Another child approached me with a bracelet they had made by threading wooden beads – they wanted me to wear it, so I took it and said thank you. "You're welcome!" they chirped.

---

[*] Carol Dweck's research published in her 2006 book 'Mindset' explains (amongst many other things) how the language we use with our children is vitally important in securing positive life outcomes. There's a pocket guide that I HIGHLY recommend! I think the government should send it home with all new parents ☺ It's called, simply, *Growth Mindset pocketbook*.

I remember being stunned: I didn't 'expect' tiny children to speak so eloquently and confidently. That day shifted the lens through which I viewed children's potential irrevocably. It was time to stop the ridiculous, over-zealous jazz-hands every time my daughter sat in her car-chair or ate a pea, which, though fashionable at the time, was ultimately exhausting for everyone and, evidently counter-productive. Here's the rub – it was difficult! I'd made one heck of a rod for my own back; I'd got her hooked on praise. The Montessori nursery I had accidentally stumbled across and fortuitously knocked on the door of, opened my eyes to a radical new approach to parenting and teaching that had, unbeknown to little-old-me, been around for donkey's years – Maria Montessori[*] was born in 1870 and she rocked.

Don't get me wrong – my children (the three indoors) are not angels. You should see their bedrooms right now. They are far from tidy. They enjoy being creative (see buttons, ribbons, paint and glue all over their respective bedroom floors). Some (my husband) might say they are messy, but others (me) can see they are mid-project and should be given space to create. They have busy lives and shifting priorities, BUT they know how to tidy and hang up clothes and when it *has* to be their priority. When you are one of thirty and it's time for PE, you need to know it's your priority to get changed quickly and you need the skills with which to do just that. Otherwise, you will face the wrath of some very angry caterpillars!

---

[*] Do yourself a favour and spend half an hour or so researching Montessori. 'How to Raise an Amazing Child the Montessori Way' by Tim Seldon, is an easy read that has graced my shelves for years.

Be part of a team

This one can be an absolute heartbreaker. There are varying degrees of adjustment that have to be made here. Learning you are not the centre of the universe is something every child goes through – it's a perfectly normal developmental process; it's part and parcel of EYFS life. Being a team player and getting changed for PE when, actually, all you want to do is play in the sand is incredibly tough. When you're not hungry and everyone is saying it's time for lunch, naturally, you question your life and the 'madness' you've been thrust into!

For a few children, however, the process of learning your place in the world is cruelly exacerbated by parental choices. When parents adopt heavily child-centric approaches to raising children, the fall out when their children start school can be devastating. There are degrees of child-centric parenting: it's a real hot potato! Some parents think running children around to a host of different clubs at the expense of family downtime is an utterly preposterous notion, whilst others fervently believe that is their duty as parents. It's contentious. There are no wrongs or rights and every family, indeed every child, is different. I celebrate that everyone is free to make their choices, and power to anyone who finds an approach to parenting that suits them and their family, but be warned: strictly child-centric parenting does not work well in conjunction with main-stream primary education because the children have unrealistic expectations of what school should be. And why wouldn't they? Imagine their confusion, anxiety and disorientation when they discover their expectations are patently not their new reality.

> A child raised in a strictly child-centric environment would understandably expect school to be a place where they choose what to learn, how to learn, when to learn and how their progress should be measured.
>
> **STAFFROOM SECRET**

Indulge me whilst I tell you a little story… When I was pregnant with my eldest, I read everything I could lay my hands on to do with pregnancy and birth. I had plans, schedules, ideals and protocols; drawers full of baby-grows, washed and ready to go; I'd decorated the nursery (I wallpapered it – first and last time in my life that's ever going to happen); I had her name (Emily) and a steadfast determination to be the best mum on planet earth. She was never going to use a dummy and, naturally (without question), I'd breastfeed. My rose-tinted glasses were well and truly superglued to my vulnerable, wide-eyes. Then she was born: BOOM*. Every aspiration and protocol went out the window; nothing went to plan. Most of the baby-grows had to be cut to accommodate the little splint she had on her arm; I could not breastfeed (no matter how hard I bit down on the flannels to struggle through the searing pain);

---

* This is an example of onomatopoeia – a word that imitates or resembles a sound. Other examples: sizzle, cuckoo. It's a tricky word to spell. If you sing the letters O N O M A T O P O E I A to the tune of 'Old Mc Donald had a farm, e-i-e-i-o', it helps!

she didn't even look like an Emily! We named her Bethany[*]
and she would not settle without a dummy. The only thing
that held up as it should was that blasted wallpaper!

I had encountered a stark reality, unyielding to my
primal, motherly desires. I was facing cold, hard facts. It was
far from perfect. But how could this be? I soon realised no
matter how perfect I IMAGINED her life should be, no
matter how much I fought and wished to protect and
nurture her, ACTUAL life was going to happen, regardless.
Love, it transpired, was no match for reality. This child was
going to have to learn fast, but I had to learn faster: lesson
one – life is not fair. I had to confess, *I'm here for you, beautiful
girl, but I'll be honest, I'm kind of just doing my best given the
circumstances. You'll have to work with me if we're going to get through
this kiddo!*

Just as life is far from perfect, schools are far from
perfect too. There is no utopian primary school where each
and every child can be catered for as individuals, with every
facet of their complex little lives being taken into account.
Our teaching superheroes are part of a school system which
is a huge, greasy cog, in a massive wheel that drives a
stinking great big truck, which chugs along a polluted
motorway through the middle of a beautiful field called life.

I understand the desire to place your child at the
centre of your life; the primal urge to protect and enable
them – to feed their curiosity and support their quest for

---

[*] I hope this goes some way to explaining why I constantly muddled up the
names of two exquisitely adorable yet wholly individual young ladies in my Year
5 class, who went by the names of Bethany and Emily. Sorry girls – I know it
drove you potty!

discovery by accompanying them wherever their natural, innate inquisitiveness may take them. However, if you want to be strictly child-centric, look ahead! Are you wearing rose-tinted spectacles? Quickly, take them off – they may make you dangerously short-sighted. If you choose, or stumble into, child-centric parenting, please plan for an education outside of the greasy cog, in the wheel of the truck, for everyone's sake.

Our school-aged children need to be equipped to deal with their realities, not our utopian fantasies. As I have stated, there are many elements to our educational system which I struggle to understand, but moaning about the system isn't going to help the four-year-old who is living and breathing 'the system' on a daily basis. What's going to help is equipping them with the tools to master the greasy cog, so they can at least enjoy the ride in the big truck! I have friends who lean heavily (if not entirely) towards a child-centric approach to parenting. They home educate or have chosen alternative educational paths for their children, and I applaud them – they have happy, healthy children being raised in arguably enviable environments. They also have key skills, time, unbridled passion, a sufficient budget, supportive networks of like-minded friends, self-discipline and the LEA (local education authority) making regular checks. I take my hat off to them.

Schools are (whether we like to admit it or not) institutions – albeit beautiful, inspiring, love-filled ones – but institutions nonetheless. Institutions rely on a heck of a lot of team playing to function harmoniously. Remember, school is far removed from the kitchen table. The same rules apply to school as to life; it's like I said to Beth (not Emily!), *You'll have to work with me if we're going to get through this kiddo!* We've all got to work together: superheroes, parents and children alike. We need to sing from the same hymn sheet. I don't mean we all have to sing the same tune – I love a harmony, and there's room for plenty in any school ('you be you' and all that); let's just endeavour to get through the song as melodically as possible. I implore you: if you cannot envisage taking on the role of full-time educator for your child, and if you want them to go to school and thrive, do not raise them in a strictly child-centric home. The discord this can create, as many superheroes sadly testify, can be simply unbearable.

Swings, roundabouts and emotional rollercoasters

Coping with our emotions is a life-long learning curve, full of those proverbial ups and downs. For children, frustrations caused by confusing feelings can be significantly relieved by simply having the ability to name them: sad, angry, jealous... There are books and flashcards on the market that will help your children recognise their emotions, and some go further by helping children understand how their emotions can link to physical symptoms (tummy ache, racing heart, nausea). Florence and I enjoyed: *The Way I Feel,* by Janan Cain. Starting 'Big School' can trigger a wealth of emotional responses, so 'dib, dib, dib' (as they said in the cubs) and be prepared. If you have already started your journey, be assured – it is never too late to go back. By understanding their emotions a little better, children recognize them in others and empathise accordingly; this is key to developing their emotional intelligence and ensuring they are capable of caring and being kind.

Food for thought

I know we've all heard it before: you are what you eat, food is fuel… Why don't we listen? I have to make myself food rotas and write inspirational quotes on my blackboard about good food and why it's so important, or I end up eating biscuits by the barrel load and feeding junk to my children! I read *Helping Your Child with Extreme Picky Eating*[*] when I was having problems with Flo, and, more recently, I watched the documentary *The Magic Pill*, which Beth recommended, and I found it fascinating. Our mood, energy levels, attention span and cognitive processing are all impacted by what we put in our mouths. Food is so powerful. I've come to realise it is my medicine or my poison. I know how difficult it can be to deal with a child who is struggling to eat well. The book and the documentary helped me; they made me feel less alone and empowered me to drive meaningful change. If you are struggling, I wish you well on your journey to better nourishment.

On your marks, get set, go!

Children typically have an abundance of energy! They need to use it. If they don't, we can't expect them to sit still and concentrate in class. It's a simple equation but sometimes (guilty as charged) we can overlook this fundamental truth. Ask yourself, have I built in energy-burning activities this weekend? For us, that doesn't mean football, ballet, karate or cheerleading – it's a long dog-walk along the blustery beach or a game of hide and seek in the dunes or a trip to the local park. If you're lucky enough to

---

[*] Jenny McGlothlin MS SLP and Katja Rowell M.D

have a garden, get out there and kick a ball or make up an obstacle course... Children love spending time with you. They'll take *quality* time with you over an iPad or TV show every time. That's one advantage of our modern 'catch-up' world – they can have it all: time with you burning energy, increased fitness and mental wellbeing *and* the latest episode of Horrible Histories. Win, win, win.

I HEARD IT THROUGH THE GRAPEVINE

The school gate (and other virtual gatherings)

On the face of it, this should be very straight forward: get to the 'gate' on time to drop off in the morning and pick up in the afternoon. If you're going to be late, just let someone know – life happens, sometimes being late is unavoidable. If you are consistently late, stop it! Your poor child bears the brunt. Get up earlier, leave sooner – none of this is rocket science, yet I cannot think of a class that has not been adversely affected by persistent latecomers, which is pretty unfortunate. Let's move on.

For some children, the school gate is the source of some serious anxiety. Leaving the safety of their home for the unfamiliar, often challenging world of school can be daunting or even paralysing. Schools are used to this. If your child is suffering from such anxieties be sure to let the school know – don't try to struggle on without support. The school needs to work with you and your child to help them feel at ease. In the cases I have witnessed, the quicker the problem is addressed, the quicker it is defused and successfully resolved.

We've established that school can be a greasy cog at times, and so, inevitably, issues will arise that need to be addressed. If you want to protect your child from all such issues, do not send them to school! Playground disputes, differences of opinion, grudges held, down-right vile behaviour, who is playing what with whom and when, etc., are a MAJOR part of any given school day. However upsetting, unfortunate or regrettable you may think this is, such 'run-ins' are instrumental in teaching our children valuable life lessons in how to deal with tricky interpersonal relationships and disputes. Arguably then, how we (parents) respond to them is hugely important. To respond effectively, we need to understand we have some explosive superpowers that need careful management before they can be successfully harnessed and implemented.

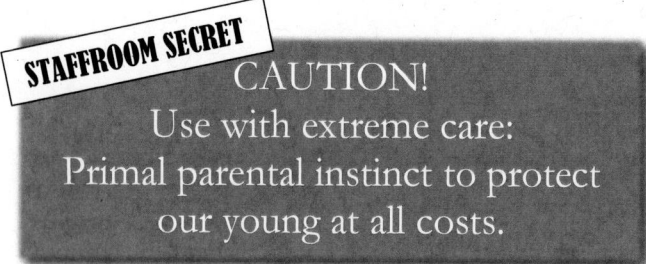

STAFFROOM SECRET

> CAUTION!
> Use with extreme care:
> Primal parental instinct to protect
> our young at all costs.

This instinct can lead to a whole host of gnarly problems. Otherwise perfectly delightful human beings become irrational, vengeful monsters with a thirst for justice, when their six-year-old comes home in tears because of a wrongdoing at school. The incredible hulk has nothing over a parent with a distraught child on their hands. I know – I've been that parent. I'm still that parent! I was that parent, yesterday, at 4:15 pm. A kind of hot flush rushes through me. I feel an urge to unleash a tirade – to vanquish the source of my child's undoing. *How dare they? Why would they? If I could have been there, I'd have…!* You get the idea. The trick is to take a breath and encourage the monster to step back. You can let it out later, in a safe space, with a trusted sounding board *far* removed from the school… A measured, constructive response is necessary – I appreciate how difficult that is when the core of your being is baying for vengeance, but a disproportionate response driven by primal parenting will only lead to further upset. Unnecessarily involving others at school can quickly spiral out of control, leading to the creation of a baying pack with their sights set on the downfall of an unwitting, defenceless six-year-old. You may think I'm exaggerating – I wish I were – but I'm not. Six-year-olds vilified. Six-year-olds and younger labelled as trouble, or worse. The 'kid to steer clear of', the one other children are encouraged to 'stay away from'. It is my fervent, unshaken belief that every child, no matter how challenging, deserves the compassion and understanding of the adults around them. If your child is struggling with another's challenging behaviour, remember that you are the compassionate adult in the equation, not the incredible hulk or another child. Work with the school. Support your child with phrases like:

READ WITH YOUR CHILD

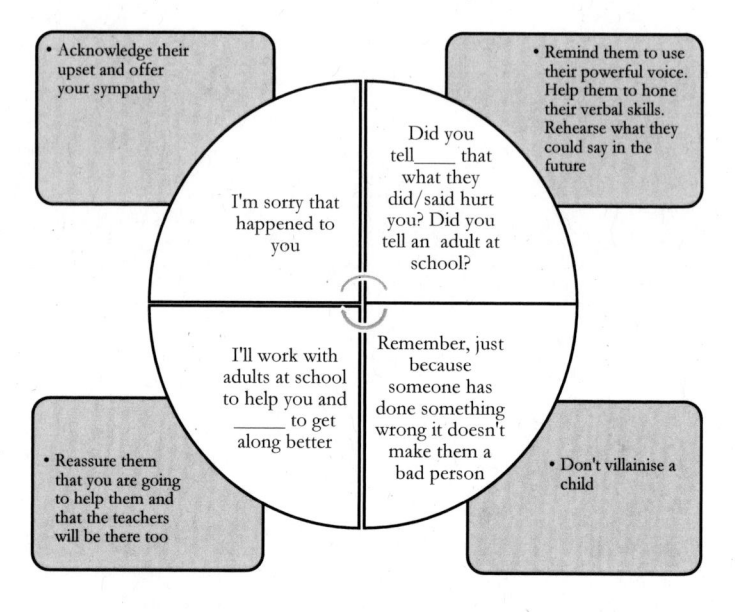

- Acknowledge their upset and offer your sympathy

- Remind them to use their powerful voice. Help them to hone their verbal skills. Rehearse what they could say in the future

- Reassure them that you are going to help them and that the teachers will be there too

- Don't villainise a child

I'm sorry that happened to you

Did you tell ____ that what they did/said hurt you? Did you tell an adult at school?

I'll work with adults at school to help you and ____ to get along better

Remember, just because someone has done something wrong it doesn't make them a bad person

Ranting and raving and declaring the child in question a juvenile delinquent will do no good in the long run. Your child has to spend the next X-number of years in the company of this child – it makes sense to build bridges, not knock them down. Let your child see the actions and hear the words of a sensible, level-headed, rational human-being when dealing with troublesome situations. Never forget – they are learning how to behave from you. Every word you utter will be heard – even those under your breath! Don't label a child a trouble-maker or, worse still, bad; you have no idea what they may be dealing with at home. Be compassionate, always. One of Lottie's dearest, kindest, gentlest, most trust-worthy friends thumped her in Year 5. It was the talk of the town! All the parents knew about it and were, frankly, a little outraged. If I'd over-reacted and warned Lottie never to go near her again, if I'd labelled that girl and fed the weed of hatred Lottie would be all the poorer... The school obviously dealt with the situation, and I was mindful not to blow it out of proportion but support Lottie through what was undoubtedly a difficult time. There are a host of storybooks to support the idea of positive, healthy friendships. I've enjoyed: *Have You Filled a Bucket Today? The Rainbow Fish,* and *Big Friends*, but there are plenty out there, aimed at different ages. For adults, I think it's worth taking a look at (or listening to) The *Chimp Paradox* by Professor Steve Peters. It explores our primal responses (the ones that make us act like chimps instead of parents).

If a particular child has been causing problems, resist the urge to ask, "What did *so-and-so* get up to today?" the moment your child gets out of school. In my experience, it can encourage children to dwell on what might otherwise be a 'minor' incident and catastrophise or even 'create' events to please you or satisfy your understandable concern and interest. Just ask how their day went...if something genuinely troubled them, in all probability, they will tell you. If you make a conscious effort to be calm and level in your responses to them, they will tell you what matters and not feel the need to hide anything from you, for fear of causing upset. Make sure they know you can handle their problems because you are the adult. Even if you are a little shaken or unsure, there is nothing to be gained from sharing that with them because it will be unsettling. They need you to be steady because they are standing on your shoulders. Take advise from trusted family, friends and teachers. Make sure you don't fall foul of catastrophising either; keep everything in perspective. That is easier said than done when your children are at the centre of your frame of reference (it's hard to see past their upset) but simply being aware of your 'skewed' vision means you will harness your emotions and move forward more productively.

Bullying

Bullying is different to a spell of upset or the odd unfortunate event. There is no legal definition of bullying; however, it's usually defined as:

> Behaviour that is repeated, intended to hurt someone either physically or emotionally – often aimed at certain groups, for example because of race, religion, gender or sexual orientation
>
> *https://www.gov.uk/bullying-at-school/bullying-a-definition

STAFFROOM SECRET

A child may become vulnerable to bullying because of something as benign as the football team they support. Understanding the difference between a playground spat and bullying is very important. Unfortunately, some parents rush to accuse another child of bullying, when it simply is not the case; this can be very difficult to deal with when parents are fuelled by their primal instinct to protect their young. Some playground issues can be long-running but still not constitute bullying. If, however, your child is the victim of bullying (bearing in mind the definition), your school should support you. For further guidance on this, visit the website: https://www.gov.uk/bullying-at-school/bullying-a-definition

Special needs on the playground

Some children, with social/emotional/behavioural difficulties, find playtime the most challenging time of day. In the classroom there are clear rules and structure, and everyone knows who's boss! On the playground the free-for-all can leave some children in a vulnerable position; the social niceties and sub-textual language of friendship, which most of us are fortunate to learn without explicit teaching, present as a veritable minefield to some. A child with social/emotional/behavioural challenges to overcome may *inadvertently* upset other children – they may lash out or shout, or perhaps sulk and cry if they do not get their own way. This behaviour, although often repeated over several years, is not the same as bullying. It can be extremely upsetting, and it's worth ensuring the school are keeping a log to document incidents, so necessary interventions can be put in place to help the children affected. Children on the receiving end of behaviour demonstrated by a child with social/emotional/behavioural difficulties will need structured support from their superheroes and you. Make sure you work with the school to ensure the most positive outcomes. Keep calm, persist, schedule regular diarised updates and ensure dialogues at home are positive – don't feed the weed!

Your child will get things wrong

Sometimes your child (yes, your angel!) will be the cause of an upset. Children make mistakes, just as adults do; it's what they are supposed to do – it's how they learn. So, if you get called over at the school gate (or by email), be aware of the three pitfalls perfectly intelligent, rational parents fall into:

Denial	Disproportionate response	Labelling your child
• It's a classic. Be open to the fact that your child could have done something wrong. No one is perfect.	• Don't vilify your child. I've seen parents who expect their children to be perfect angels and chastise them mercilessly. The odd misdemeanour is to be expected. Your child is human – just like you.	• Labelling your child instead of the act. "You are so naughty!" instead of "Snatching the food was naughty." Never tell your child they are naughty/bad/stupid etc. they'll start to believe you and act accordingly.

The red mist

In the course of your child's primary education, you can expect there to be times when you do not see eye-to-eye with your child's superhero. Be aware that just as other children can bring out your incredible hulk, so too can a superhero you perceive to have wronged your child. Take a breath. Do not get on your soapbox on the school gate or social media platform of your choice. The school will inevitably hear about it. Someone always tells a member of staff, forwards a link, screenshots a page, drops us an email. You may think your chat room is private – I've been shown countless 'private/closed group' discussions and threads. This may sound dramatic but unwitting parents can find themselves faced with defamation of character charges hanging over them because of a hot-tempered, primal-parent, prosecco fuelled rant on social media. If you have a grievance, arrange a meeting to discuss it – there are always two sides to all disputes and, as you are not at school, you need to be informed of the context. I urge you not to write inflammatory emails before you are in possession of ALL the facts, not just your child's version of events, as they live on and leave a sour taste in the mouths of those who dedicate their careers to enriching the lives of children. More often than not, something we as parents have stewed over turns out to be nothing more than a misunderstanding, miscommunication or minor incident that, when in possession of all the facts and mitigating circumstances, can be easily resolved. I often joke with parents from my class:

> If you don't believe everything your child says happens at school, I won't believe everything they say happens at home!
>
> **STAFFROOM SECRET**

Children's perceptions are far from sophisticated or refined; misunderstandings are, therefore, relatively commonplace. Be aware that angry parents come across as threatening and aggressive. Keep your emotions in check – threatening behaviour cannot be tolerated in our schools. You may have had challenging relationships with your teachers in the past – you are not dealing with those teachers now – leave your baggage outside the door.

Of course, it could well be that your child's superhero has made a mistake – just as you have made countless mistakes as a parent… I trust you have found it in your heart to forgive yourself your parenting mistakes. I always justify my parenting mistakes to myself: I was tired, I misread the situation, I've got three very demanding children and I was frazzled that day, I had a banging headache… I imagine you recognise some of those. Teachers are human, just like parents – give them a break. I had 32 children in my last class, and, although I did my very best, sometimes I got things wrong. I'm not superhuman; I'm a superhero – there's a difference! Unless it's serious, repeated, detrimental to your child's development, dangerous etc. please realise (and help your child to realise) that actually, it might not be such a big deal after all. Ranting at the gate or on social media will never make anything better. Talk to your child's teacher if you feel it necessary – just please remember to ask yourself the question, 'Is this really necessary?'. If the answer is yes – go ahead.

I'm afraid to say some parents feel it 'necessary' to talk to the teacher *every day*! If you know a parent like that, I beg you, tell them to stop it. If you are that parent, for the love of all things primary, please, stop it. It's exhausting. No one will ever take you seriously when it actually matters. The same rules apply to the office staff. Do not plague the office with questions you could easily find the answers to on the school website or by reading correspondence that's been sent home. The office staff are *incredibly* busy running a school and are not there for our convenience.

The power is in your hands

If you do have serious concerns, call every meeting you need to, get the governors involved, contact the local authority or trust – protect your child. You have great power as a parent, and you should never shy away from using it should the genuine need arise.

STAFFROOM SECRET

> The school gate and social media is not the place to resolve any issues – always go through the appropriate channels.

If you hear someone airing a grievance, have the wherewithal to excuse yourself from the conversation. Don't fuel the fire! If you are feeling really brave, venture to suggest they'd be better off talking to the school. Remember, whatever you hear from other parents is their version of events; their perspective will be informed by all sorts of factors. Crucially, you are hearing one side of a story. Listening to unsubstantiated opinions or versions of events and taking that as 'gospel' is clearly not what anyone should be doing; repeating what you have heard and lending it credence is even worse.

Finally, when you collect your child from the gate, ask them what went well today – find out what was amazing or wonderful about their day. Ask them to teach you something they learned. Celebrate their little triumphs and commiserate with them when they stumble. Listen intently to what we as grown-ups often think of as painfully dull detail – it may seem like small stuff to us but it's BIG to them. They need to learn that you're interested and listening, so that, as they become older, they feel comfortable to tell you the *really* big stuff…

VIDEO KILLED THE RADIO STAR

I feel this chapter should come with a warning. I am going to get passionate. I am looking through the lens of a teacher and speaking from horrid experience and rising frustration. I will be animated, but please read this chapter and try to understand that I am speaking from my heart and with the very best of intentions. I want to protect you from the embarrassment (at best) or heartbreak you'll feel if you fail to protect your children online.

STAFFROOM SECRET

The guidelines state:

NO PRIMARY AGED CHILDREN SHOULD BE USING SOCIAL MEDIA.

Computing is part and parcel of our children's lives both at home and at school. Primary schools teach computing, and included in the syllabus is a healthy dose of internet safety lessons. Given the amount of advice we send out to adults regarding internet safety, a significant number of parents are still unaware of the guidelines in place to protect their children. Undeterred, I would like, with the help of Action for Children, to reiterate:

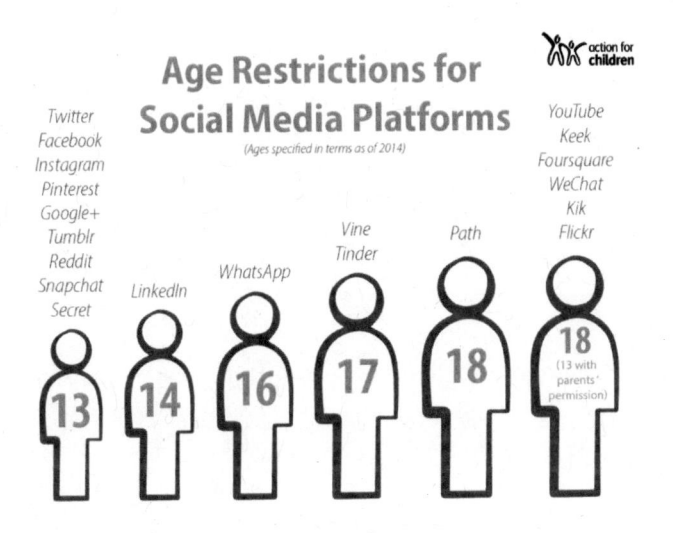

Age Restrictions for Social Media Platforms
(Ages specified in terms as of 2014)

action for children

- 13: Twitter, Facebook, Instagram, Pinterest, Google+, Tumblr, Reddit, Snapchat, Secret
- 14: LinkedIn
- 16: WhatsApp
- 17: Vine, Tinder
- 18: Path
- 18 (13 with parents' permission): YouTube, Keek, Foursquare, WeChat, Kik, Flickr

There are different ages for different accounts – Facebook and Twitter, for example, recommend 13 as a minimum age to have an account, whilst WhatsApp recommend 16. Some guidelines changed when GDPR became a part of our lives.

Because of my responsibility to safeguard the children in my care, I obviously cannot share, in any detail, the numerous, serious issues I have dealt with regarding the misuse of social media platforms. Children from loving, conscientious families have found themselves in a whole world of trouble because they have inadvertently stumbled into a situation without their parents' knowledge. Suddenly, the child (who invariably knows they should not have been on the site in the first place) is too ashamed or embarrassed to seek the help they need. All too often, the responsible adults are either totally unaware their children are using the sites, or they have given their consent (assuming it will be harmless) grossly underestimating the danger they are putting their children in. I'll attempt to paraphrase and amalgamate the things I have heard parents say when social media has bitten back: "I can't believe it; I'm beyond shocked; I trusted them explicitly; this is not like them at all; they have never done anything like this before; how could they have been so stupid?" What always amazes me is that parents truly believe they can just 'trust' their child; they believe their offspring is going to be the first human on the planet never to make a stupid mistake! And what I find unfathomable is that even if they trust their *saintly child* do they really trust the other 7.8 billion strangers on the planet? To my mind, letting an eight-year old loose on YouTube to post videos for the world to comment on is asking for big trouble. We've done searches at school before – we've simply typed in names of children in our classes to see what comes up. It's terrifying. Then there are the late-night revelations. One diligent parent will spot a chat on an iPad left open one morning, only to discover a group of children have been up until the small hours (usually waffling on about a lot of harmless nonsense) undetected by their parents, who all claim to have a handle on the social media usage in their households. As the teacher, I am then informed, and I have to sort it all out. Frankly, it's getting harder to hear the excuses and apologies. When children are tired and distracted and underachieve because of a lack of sleep (which has often gone undetected for a considerable length of time), it's horribly frustrating. Please, please stick to the guidelines for everyone's sakes. Don't allow devices in their rooms at night. Help us to help them.

If you are lucky, the misuse will be minimal – perhaps your child will be upset by comments posted about them, or unhappy about a photo they are not keen on being shared. It is not uncommon, however, for hurtful comments to spiral out of control in an unsupervised, virtual environment. This can escalate to become cyberbullying, which has serious implications and impacts on a child's mental health and wellbeing.

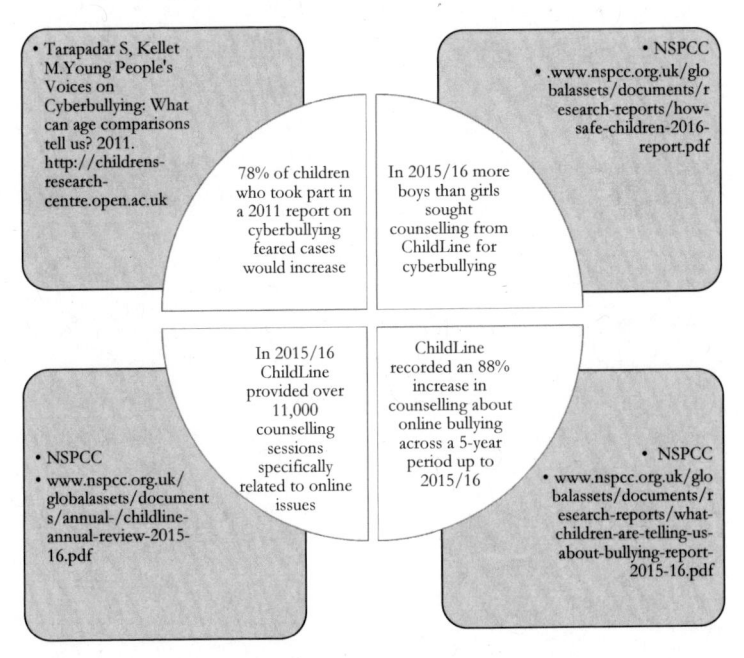

- Tarapadar S, Kellet M.Young People's Voices on Cyberbullying: What can age comparisons tell us? 2011. http://childrens-research-centre.open.ac.uk

78% of children who took part in a 2011 report on cyberbullying feared cases would increase

In 2015/16 more boys than girls sought counselling from ChildLine for cyberbullying

- NSPCC
- .www.nspcc.org.uk/globalassets/documents/research-reports/how-safe-children-2016-report.pdf

- NSPCC
- www.nspcc.org.uk/globalassets/documents/annual-/childline-annual-review-2015-16.pdf

In 2015/16 ChildLine provided over 11,000 counselling sessions specifically related to online issues

ChildLine recorded an 88% increase in counselling about online bullying across a 5-year period up to 2015/16

- NSPCC
- www.nspcc.org.uk/globalassets/documents/research-reports/what-children-are-telling-us-about-bullying-report-2015-16.pdf

The damage done by misuse of internet browsing platforms and social media apps can be utterly devastating. It is not uncommon for children to need counselling, and sometimes the social services and the police have to be involved. What worries me most is that those are the cases we know about...what about all the others? Don't make the mistake of thinking it won't happen to you. All children make mistakes, they make bad choices, and they can be cunning and secretive if they feel they need to be.

Talk to your child about being safe online. Make sure that when they are searching the internet, you are there too. Check to ensure you have parental locks on your devices and be in no hurry to furnish your child with a phone. Despite what they may well be telling you, it is not the case that 'Everyone else has got one!' If they need a phone because of travel or family dynamics, make sure it is just that: a phone. If they only need to make calls and perhaps send a text message, they do not need all the bells and whistles!

On the whole, the internet is a bright light, illuminating our children's world with information and entertainment, but wherever there is light there are shadows. In the darkest of those shadows hide the most dangerous people. The strangers who pose the biggest threat are those who pretend to be who they are not, in order to harm our children. Every child is vulnerable.

Gaming, films and television

Another significant problem affecting our primary-aged children is inappropriate gaming and the viewing of age-inappropriate films/TV series. It is not uncommon for superheroes to be presented with bleary-eyed children who have been up until the small hours playing online games with their friends. Most of us have seen traumatised children who have been exposed to explicit, graphic content from films or games. Seeing tiny children behaving inappropriately on the playground, acting out what they have seen on a gaming console (played by an adult in their house) is no longer a surprise. We've dealt with children who've had sleepless nights from glimpses of horror films or troubled thoughts from films they have streamed, unnoticed by the adults in the house. Of course, when these issues arise, and parents are invited to school to discuss matters further, it is never a pleasant conversation. In the vast majority of these cases, the parents are utterly (genuinely) shocked and horrified that it has happened to *their* child. Screen safety is an issue for ALL families. Think about your child's wider world; they could be exposed (for example) on a playdate or sleepover – you need to cover all bases and talk openly with your child. Work hard to create an environment where they feel they can tell you if they've seen something that has unsettled them, and protect them by implementing all the recommended safety measures in your home.

My intention here is not to scaremonger. I am simply speaking from experience and a heartfelt place of duty and responsibility. If, for whatever reason, the message has not hit home before, or your school have not communicated the seriousness of these issues, or if you have assumed your family is different (and you are somehow protected from the shadows), I implore you to listen now:

TAKE ACTION - KEEP YOUR CHILD SAFE ON **ALL TYPES OF SCREEN.** Rant over.

Given my rant, you would be forgiven for imagining my children live in a world devoid of technology because I am gripped by fear. Happily, the opposite is true! We love it. Flo goes to Tech Club and loves programming. She's made a random name generator and takes advantage of the free sessions run in our local Apple Store. As a teacher, I think what we offer in school is far from what is needed; the jobs of the future (that we are yet to imagine) are predicted to be 'tech-heavy'. I wonder how many of our children will be best placed to take advantage of these roles? If you can access any programming activities for your child, encourage them to give coding a go. Apple's *Swift Playgrounds* is a free app but doesn't work on all devices; *Scratch* is free and used in lots of schools, so it is likely to dovetail home and school learning. You could ask your school what they use in the classroom and use that as a starting point…

Radio Star

Let's just take a second to think about the 'Radio Star'. There are children's radio stations, podcasts, audiobooks and music to listen to…all of which can be enjoyed whilst they colour, draw, build or simply rest. I know what it is to be busy. I know what it is to crave an hour's peace. The age gap between my children is such that, often, Florence is like an only child and she craves company. Instead of sticking her in front of CBBC (which, incidentally, I love) I will often pop on an audio something-or-another in her room and leave her to get on with whatever she fancies. This has proved to be some of the most productive, creative, child-led playtime she has had.

So, if you had forgotten the joy of listening to a story, perhaps re-acquaint yourself with (and introduce your child to) the wonder of freeing your eyes and liberating your body from the couch. Oh, the wonder of guilt-free, hassle-free children's entertainment. Not only do I get some downtime, I get the added bonus of feeling virtuous when Florence finally emerges (often hours later) with her wondrous creation. Yesterday's tissue-paper dress, held together with mini pegs, will live on in my heart forever! Parents, we can have it all: winning at parenting whilst enjoying a cuppa – you gotta love Stephen Fry and that Potter chap!

Chart-toppers

The Chappell household has a playlist of songs to motivate and inspire us to do our best. Music is a great teacher, mentor and spiritual guide; be sure to compile a playlist of your own. Here are a few from our *School Run Fun* playlist to get you started:

Title	Artist
Bring It All Back	S Club 7
Shine	Take That
Proud	Heather Small
Unwritten	Natasha Beddingfield
Firework	Katie Perry
Wonder	Emeli Sande
Almost There	Anika Noni Rose
Reach	S Club 7
Hall of Fame	The Script
Ain't No Mountain High Enough	Marvin Gaye & Tammi Terrell
Bridge Over Troubled Water	Simon & Garfunkel
I'm Still Standing	Elton John

Try Everything	Shakira
Make Your Own Kind of Music	Paloma Faith
Happy	Pharrell Williams
Corner of the Sky	Matthew James Thomas
This Is Me	Keala Settle & The Greatest Showman
How Far I'll Go	Auli'i Cravalho
Walking on Sunshine	Katrina & The Waves

THIS IS HOW WE DO IT
How we learn – growth mindset and more

Different people learn in different ways. Some favour visual learning (pictures, drawings, graphs, etc.), whilst others prefer auditory learning (chanting their timestables, listening to a story). Some favour a kinaesthetic approach (putting actions to stories, learning their timestables by linking them to movements). Some enjoy working in groups, and others work better in solitude. In every class, there are learners who are mainly logical (they think in a linear fashion) and are typically comfortable with abstract concepts, like a list of equations for example. There will also be plenty who struggle with the abstract and linear – those who create a 'web' of ideas and concepts to learn something new. Of course, no child learns exclusively in one way, and preferences can change – it's important not to label or pigeonhole our children. As a superhero, it's my job to 'mix-it-up'. I can't pander to everyone's preferences – it would be chaos. Besides, children who prefer to work in solitude need to learn how to work with groups and vice versa, to prepare them for life in the real world.

The brain is like a muscle: the more we train it the stronger and more effective it becomes. By working across the brain (left to right) and 'mixing it up', more of the brain is stimulated, which helps neural pathways form. It's essentially a better workout. The stronger the neural pathway, the more secure our understanding is. When children are really struggling with a concept, a superhero will (of course) go to that child's 'preferred style' to help them grasp on, but once they are holding tightly, it's beneficial to explore the concept in as many ways as possible. In my class, I make a conscious effort to teach the children in as many ways as I can. Having a boogie in Year 5 maths is standard, as is making a factor bug (complete with springy legs), doing an online Christmas shop, working on the promotion material for a start-up Mexican restaurant, playing cards, throwing dice, drawing equations, creating beautiful art from 2D shapes and composing complex cross-rhythms from clapping fractions! It's all about strengthening those neural pathways and having FUN! If you have fun, you relax, and learning happens as if by accident. Anxious children, who feel pressure to learn, will be unable to as their bodies switch to 'fight, flight, freeze' mode. Consequently, their brains are simply switched off from learning to deal with the more pressing matter of surviving, which can be terribly upsetting, embarrassing and even humiliating.

Stop press! My Beth tells me that blueberries, dark chocolate and crunchy food help your brain to build its neural pathways[*]. Get munching, people!

The benefits of having fun with learning are something I cannot overstate. It seems blatantly obvious, yet so many parents tell me about the tears and tantrums they encounter at home when they try to tackle homework. If your child is traumatised when trying to learn – STOP. You'll need to approach whatever it is later but from a completely different angle. More on homework trials and tribulations later…there's a chapter on the subject. I'll need to find some steps (or a whopping great-big ladder), so I can safely mount my incredibly high horse to write it! For now, though, let's continue to focus on how we can help our children to learn. Fun, fun, fun…self-motivated, curiosity-fuelled learning is not only the most enjoyable it's the most effective. I've just got home from picking up Lottie from school – it's a Saturday, but she went in (voluntarily) to a pre-GCSE English Literature session because the exam is in 3 days. Lottie loves her English teacher. "She doesn't tell us 'This means this, that means that…' She says, 'What do you think? What do you reckon the writer's up to here?' We have a good old natter about it." It's funny – of all the lessons Lottie has, this superhero sets the least homework and does not set strict deadlines when she does. She has created a space where the children feel safe to question her, express their opinions and even (shock horror) openly disagree with her. The same superhero taught the girls'

---

[*] Sandrine Thuret, neuroscientist TED talk
https://www.ted.com/talks/sandrine_thuret_you_can_grow_new_brain_cells_here_s_how/transcript?language=en#t-514865

English Language curriculum last year. The whole year group took that exam and RS a year early, to ease the burden this year. Lottie's class smashed it! I mean, they topped national charts... This particular undercover superhero had conjured such a trick – Lottie (who had failed her 11+ and had been predicted a 5 at GCSE English Language) got a 9. For those of you who have yet to master the new and arguably utterly ridiculous GCSE grading system, that's the top mark possible. We're talking A**. I know this is anecdotal but let's face it there are *lies, damn lies and statistics*, and this kind of superhero power is hard to quantify in a spreadsheet.

Growth Mindset – have you got yours YET?

For a brain to learn effectively, it needs a bit of help. It needs its owner to be aware of what a GROWTH MINDSET is. I am passionate about the power of instilling our children with a growth mindset because I have seen the remarkable (nay, gob-smacking) difference it can make. I worked with a superhero colleague on an action research project relating to girls' attainment in mathematics, and the results were startling. For me, the bedrock of teaching is in a growth mindset approach.

Time for another story... When I was sixteen, I sat in a taster A-level sociology session which explored the labelling theory and the self-fulfilling prophecy. I was stunned to discover that perhaps the reason I had failed my maths was that my mum had told me not to fret about my innate short-comings (it was genetic – she couldn't do it either). Hang on a minute – my teachers had done it too! They always put me in the lowest set (they called it the Blue

Set, but we all knew what that meant). Dancing, on the other hand, had been something both mum and dad thought I'd excel in. I could tap away in time to the music as a young dot, and they could both 'cut-a-rug'. Dad had been a professional athlete – this was looking promising. They drove me across Kent to the best dance school in the area. I went dancing at least three times a week (I was there all day on Saturdays). I entered competitions (which I hated!), trained for exams (which I dreaded) and was told by my parents that I had a gift! Funnily enough, after all that practise, I was pretty good. Had I been labelled? Had I self-fulfilled my mother's prophecy? I was flipping cross – why hadn't someone mentioned this voodoo earlier? A lot earlier. I was sixteen now – my life was basically over!

Remembering this revelation, many years later (life it seemed was not over), I was inspired to read Carol Dweck's book on growth mindset because, from what I'd heard, it bore striking similarities to the labelling theory and self-fulfilling prophecy I'd been told about. To whet your appetite and inspire you to read more, (in a crude nutshell) Dweck exposes the shortcomings of parents and teachers who praise results instead of the process or effort required to reach an end result. There are countless examples in her book and Matthew Syed's book: *Bounce*, of inspirational, successful people who have benefitted from a growth mindset. The opposite of a growth mindset is a fixed one – where you believe intelligence is pre-determined at birth. A person with a fixed mindset avoids failure, avoids challenge, sticks to what they know and takes personal offence when given feedback. Someone with a growth mindset embraces challenge, sees failure as key to learning, piles in effort and seeks feedback – often learning from others. Some people are very much one or the other – some are a mix of the two, depending on the situation they find themselves in. What is key, however, is our ability to BECOME an individual with a GROWTH MINDSET by working at it. Schools up and down the country have latched onto this because they have seen how children's emotional wellbeing and consequently their results have been positively affected. However, schools cannot teach this alone – they need parents and families to join in too. After all, these are our children's most influential teachers. If the school is embracing a growth mindset approach but you are asking your child, 'Who is the cleverest at maths?' horribly mixed messages will confuse and muddy the waters.

Huge potential can underperform

Parents are often surprised when I warn that high-achieving children are susceptible to falling into the fixed mindset very early on in their development. If told by beaming, proud adults how 'bright, talented, gifted and clever' they are, children can quickly fear being seen as anything less – for fear of upsetting those who clearly *value* them for their innate gifts. Oh, the pressure must be unbearable. They daren't fail. Mistakes feel like such disasters. They hide misunderstandings for fear of being found out and shy away from asking questions. These 'bright, talented, clever' children will most likely plateau early and achieve less than their full potential. The poor things – what a burden these labels can be. Undoing the damage labelling children can cause is sometimes a very tricky task indeed, which is why they are best avoided in the first place. However, it is never too late. I read Dweck's book when Bethany was in secondary school. I explained it all to her and apologised profusely for labelling her as clever, etc. I'd been well-meaning; I was trying to boost her self-esteem and confidence. Poor old Beth. The eldest is so often our unwitting guinea pig...however, no guilt is allowed: Jane-of-the-past was not a fortune teller!

When children get everything right in an exercise without any struggle, they are not learning; they are demonstrating what they already know. A page of ticks is not necessarily the mark of a good superhero. If I see a page of ticks (without challenge/struggle/extension), I haven't done my job properly, and I should be apologising – not handing out gold stars to the pupil and patting myself on the back. However, it's great to see a page of ticks as part of the consolidation process, when they've completed the journey and the struggle. That's when the EFFORT is praised and it's time to move on and find a new challenge.

We've seen how the fixed mindset is detrimental to children who learn quickly. What about those who are struggling? A fixed mindset can inadvertently give struggling children permission to underachieve and not reach their potential. Remember my wonderful mum and her attitude towards maths? It's not your fault; you shouldn't get so upset; we can't all be good at everything...all those loving, well-meant reassurances. Of course (with the benefit of hindsight) mum would say (and does say to the grandchildren) 'Come on love – I know you can't remember it YET but with a bit more revision you will. How could we look at this differently?' Sometimes she'll say, 'Time for a rest – it's important to know the difference between a rest and giving up!' Mum is living proof that brains are capable of change and learning new things – she's been giving fractions a go, aged seventy-three. Not bad considering she left school just before they taught her decimals.

Of course, another key factor in how we learn is who we learn from. I've made no secret of the fact I believe the significant, constant adult in a child's life is their main teacher, but don't underestimate siblings, friends, relatives and the media. Be mindful of the soft lessons your children learn from others. For example, if your dad is telling your children how talented and naturally brilliant they are, explain how that is detrimental to their progress and wellbeing. Tell him you'd really appreciate him praising the effort they have made (praise the process) and how much they'd value some constructive feedback for future improvement. Grandparents can still declare they are proud as punch – and it won't affect their bragging rights. Lottie (my sixteen-year-old) is quite the little musician: she can play the piano, violin and viola; she composes beautifully and has taken lots of formal examinations, at a relatively young age. When anyone comments and says how 'talented' she is, I waste no time in gently correcting them. I do it for Lottie – her wellbeing is my priority. I talk about the hours she spends working, how it does not come 'naturally' and about her motivation, which is derived from passion and determination. It's clear that I am as proud as can be; Lottie is still praised but for what she has done – not for having a gift bestowed unto her. If Lottie believed she had a 'gift', she'd had given up on music at grade 1, believing she'd misplaced her 'gift' somewhere down the back of the sofa…

Careful the things you say: children will listen…*

Our language is key to ensuring our children grow to meet their full potential. That said, children have strengths and weaknesses – undoubtedly, some find learning easier than others – but what I'm talking about here is POTENTIAL. Some of the most successful people were late developers with specific or multiple learning difficulties. They were successful because they worked very hard and were passionate about their field of eventual expertise. As the saying goes:

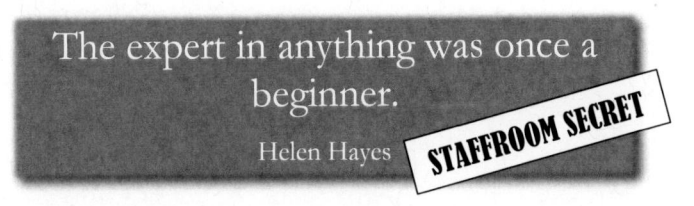

> The expert in anything was once a beginner.
> Helen Hayes

STAFFROOM SECRET

As parents, we have the power to feed enthusiasm, fuel passion, encourage our children and remove barriers by simply choosing our words carefully. What a neat trick! Move over Potter - there's a new army of wizarding parents in town with the power of YET in their cauldrons and plenty of 'PRAISE the PROCESS' potion** under their capes.

Dopamine dramas!

I think adults often idealise childhood. We have a tendency to romanticise and simplify this hugely significant

---

* Stephen Sondheim, Into The Woods
** All those P's are an example of ALLITERATION, which is in the vocabulary list. We play the ALLITERATION GAME in the car. We work alphabetically and take turns: Animated Ant, Barbequing Buffalo etc… Bonus points for 3 or 4 worders: Curious, Caterwauling, Cantankerous Cat! They are never as good as that in the car!

and formative time because we wish it were all sunshine and rainbows for our children. In reality, of course, a little rain must fall. Children encounter traumas, loss, illness, etc. just as adults do. They have social stresses, the expectations of adults to handle and their families' quirks to contend with. Childhood is not all lemonade, blue skies, picnics and bike rides, despite what Enid Blyton might have us believe.

Remember, just because a child's frame of reference is different to our own, it doesn't mean their issues are any less significant than ours. To them a playground spat is central to their world, just as a huge row with a spouse would be central to ours. It's important to recognise their frame of reference and not trivialise their concerns and worries or, indeed, their preoccupations and fascinations. I'm preoccupied by my carbon footprint and the ridiculous packaging in the supermarkets at the moment – I want to be taken seriously; Flo is preoccupied with Harry Potter, Horrible Histories and Lego – she deserves to be taken seriously too. Whilst taking our children seriously, we must also stop them from catastrophising their concerns or fixating (for example, on Harry Potter) to the point of unhealthy obsession! We have to put strategies in place to move forward constructively: talking it through, listening carefully and offering up healthy diversions to broaden their horizons. Children have all this (life!) to contend with, when suddenly (from about the age of eight) their brains are flooded with dopamine. Neurobiologist, Dr. Andrew Curran[*] uses a simple graph to illustrate the biological phenomenon that is crucial yet inherently problematic for our children. He explains that dopamine is critical for

---

[*] Brain Development – Andrew Carran. https://vimeo.com/250809215

learning, unlearning, and paying attention and works well when balanced with serotonin. However, when the dopamine far exceeds the serotonin (as it does from about age eight) it causes problems because "if your brain is full of dopamine, is flooded with dopamine, it's hyperactive; it's sitting on a level of excitation which is not functional and useful".[*]

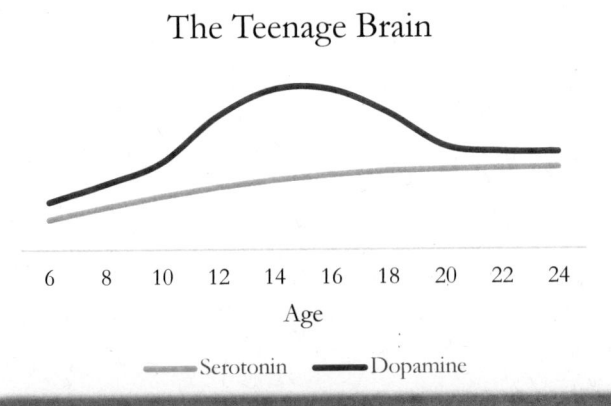

The Teenage Brain

| 6 | 8 | 10 | 12 | 14 | 16 | 18 | 20 | 22 | 24 |

Age

——— Serotonin   ——— Dopamine

> What nature wants is adolescents to take high risk decisions with poor judgement because then they achieve two critical goals: they break free of their dependence on their parents, and they learn how to interface with their peer group by trial and error, so they can become successful adults.
>
> Andrew Curran

STAFFROOM SECRET

---

[*] Brain Development – Andrew Carran. https://vimeo.com/250809215

Too much dopamine inhibits our ability to think clearly and make decisions. I hope that knowing about dopamine helps you understand why a seven-year-old who is so 'on track' can become so 'difficult' by the time they are nine... Keep calm and help them to carry on. I know how infuriating it can be, but they do have a legitimate reason for being a tad 'disengaged' at times! An astonishing 93% of dopamine secretion is directly under the control of the limbic (emotional) brain, so to support our young people we need to engage with their limbic brain. Being understood bolsters a child's self-esteem and self-confidence – it makes them engage with their emotional brain and helps them connect with their world. I guess this is at the root of why I believe parents are their children's best teachers.

> If somebody's in an environment, or with someone where they feel genuine love, then their ability to deal with themselves and their lives is maximised. And this, of course, doesn't have to be some big, profound Hollywood love – just the sense of being understood...
>
> Andrew Curran

STAFFROOM SECRET

WHAT A WONDERFUL WORLD THIS WOULD BE

I've found an extendable ladder - bring me the highest horse you can find

Time for another story. I used to think I'd be judged as a terrible parent if Beth (the eldest) didn't hand in fabulous homework, on time. From Year 1, I'd write it out first then she'd have to copy it. If it wasn't good enough, I'd make her do it again... Her projects were frankly frameworthy. I remember Beth spending many hours copying what I'd written about Africa one miserable Sunday afternoon. I thought a good mum had to go the extra mile – that we had to make sure our children worked hard. Poor, poor Beth. I bet she can't remember a thing about Africa from that blasted project. Although, one of her first jobs was working for the BBC World Service: Africa Eye, so...!

Now I'm a superhero, I understand:

> Homework is the superheroes' way of seeing how crazy the parents are!
>
> STAFFROOM SECRET

It can be hilarious. A-level standard art submitted by a child in reception (I kid you not); fluent, well-crafted paragraphs presented by the child who struggles to construct a well-ordered sentence or two (even when assisted) in class; a sheet of perfectly ordered fractions handed in by the child who proceeds to get all her equations incorrect in the lesson. So, what was the point? Who learned what, exactly?

Fast forward a few years or ten, and I'm encouraging Flo (the youngest) to write to her headteacher explaining why she'd really rather not have as much homework! She's got fun things to do in the evenings and homework is getting in the way.

Whatever the homework, remember the intention is for the child to consolidate their learning or explore something new in preparation for what lies ahead in class. They should not be doing homework to satisfy you or please the superhero because that's the wrong motivation – they should be doing it for themselves. You can use language to support this idea. I never call the girls' learning at home 'homework' – I call it home-learning. Your child's home-learning is their opportunity to grow – assisted and nurtured by you. Little and often is key. Don't let it overwhelm them.

I'll throw some ideas up in the air regarding the support of learning spellings, times-tables and reading later in the book – hang on in there! Homework (beyond spellings, times-tables and reading) should hold within it the capacity to create a spark in a child's imagination – a spark you have the power to fan and nurture, with the hope it may become a burning flame of curiosity, which leads naturally to more learning…

Some prescriptive 'learning' has to happen at home: times-tables, daily reading, non-phonetic spellings (often called tricky or 'red' words). These tasks are time-consuming, require regular repetition and often require 1:1 assistance and support. Home support is needed here to realise your child's potential. When you fail to assist, it is usually blatantly obvious. My most severely dyslexic students were capable of getting full marks in their spellings (adapted to suit their needs) when parents went all out to support them. A growth mindset was key to ensuring those fabulous results. It was not a walk in the park for those families like it was for the families of visual and logical learners. Life isn't fair my friends – it's full of greasy cogs. Mind you, the spontaneous, heartfelt celebration that always erupted in the classroom when those children reached their potential was beautiful. Their classmates were celebrating the exceptional effort they knew their friends had made.

If I were the King of the Forest*

Other than those three key disciplines: reading, times-tables and spellings, I'd abolish all other homework. I

---

* I had to get The Wizard of Oz in. My class will be delighted!

know I'm getting ideas above my station; I appreciate that I am a lowly classroom superhero, but I would heartily encourage you to challenge your school if your child is being loaded down with arduous homework tasks. They work so, so hard in school and they need to rest. Anxiety is rife among our children – fuelled by unnecessary pressures. If your child is spending longer than 30 minutes on homework (on any given day), I'd encourage you to stop them. If they are confronted with a task they do not understand, and you cannot confidently assist them, I'd implore you to make them stop. Take the matter up with your school. Calmly. There is a wealth of evidence to suggest such homework, levelled at primary school children, is wholly inappropriate, counterproductive and detrimental to our children's wellbeing.

Family-learning, however, is a whole other ball game! The distinction is subtle but important.

STAFFROOM SECRET

> The word 'family' takes the pressure off the child because it is clear this is an activity to be shared – it is not their sole responsibility.

Removing the word 'work' and replacing it with 'learning' makes it clear that this is something you are doing for your self-improvement, to enrich your life; it is not for the benefit of your superhero – you are not working for them.

In my little fantasy classroom, there would be the usual home-based tasks to complete (spellings, reading, times-tables) and then there would be family-learning. This would comprise of fun activities for families to enjoy which support what is going on in the classroom. When families have 2,3 or more children in the same school, having lots of different homework tasks to complete divides family time, puts unnecessary pressure on parents and ultimately causes stress, in what should be a place of sanctuary – our homes. I believe schools should embrace school-wide projects so that family-learning is the same for every child in the school. This would build a sense of community and encourage relationships across year groups. In assembly time, examples of family-learning could be shared to help inspire others; families could (as many of my children's families did) send in photos to be shared with the class/school. This encourages the children to learn from one another.

I'd make some family-learning weekly: aspirational vocabulary, look at a growth-mindset phrase, play a board game. These tasks are small and not time-consuming (if you don't choose Monopoly). The other tasks, which are more involved, could be half-termly enterprises so that families can plan when to do them.

Challenge the family to use an aspirational piece of vocab. It'll soon pop up in class-based writing	Choose from a list of suggested age-appropriate reading or listening (e-book)	Discuss: "Dreams don't work unless you do." (John C. Maxwell)	Play a two-diced board game: maths (number bonds) PSHE (sharing/taking turns)
Bake a cake with vegetables in: supporting maths, science and PSHE	Build a junk-model robot from the contents of your recycling	Watch a given documentary (on the rainforest, for example) in preparation for a school-wide topic	Write to the Prime Minister asking to ban homework: English (persuasive writing) and British Values (individual liberty)

I was lucky: my school embraced many of these concepts, and the homework the children used to suffer together with their parents happily became a thing of the past. Goodbye to the weekly, soul-destroying, dull comprehension – hello cooking a meal for the family, writing a thank you letter to someone who inspires you, and fitting the word 'ramshackle' into your daily life! We produced a bingo-type grid of home-learning that was well received and easily updated. Results did not suffer – in fact, quite the opposite.

I know that, sadly, some parents do not support their children with even the most basic of homework tasks. Those parents are few and far between and should come up as a 'red-flag' to superheroes, who (assisted by senior colleagues) are duty-bound to investigate why they are falling short of their parental duties. Just as being late or absent on the odd occasion is understandable, so too is failing to complete the odd piece of homework. However, consistently neglecting to support your child's learning at home is worthy of further investigation. Happily, the vast majority of parents are keen to support their children's learning, and (given the right inspiration) enjoy getting involved. If you are not inspired, and homework is a problem at your school, why not launch a peaceful, well-mannered revolution? Go on. I dare you.

You would be forgiven at this point for thinking I have lost my marbles. 'Didn't this woman start the book by saying I had to be more involved? Now she's advocating less homework!' So that I can make myself clear, we'll need to think about Lottie's English teacher – the one who magically cultivated the 'table-topping' results, in an environment rich with learning opportunities which inspired and promoted curiosity and questioning. Do you remember the Montessori goddesses? The ones who created the environment where children were given responsibility and were expected to be able, where they were gifted with that most precious commodity: time. They encouraged children to be self-motivated by providing opportunities to master skills independently. That is what I want to help you create in your homes.

A B C – EASY AS 1 2 3

"We are what we repeatedly do.
Excellence, then, is not an act but a habit."[*]

Learning anything new requires repetition. Riding a bike – remember how tricky that was? Easier for some than for others but it requires practice, right? Walking – that takes a while too… talking, swimming, doing a cartwheel! When you don't do things for a while, you get rusty. I dread to think what my cartwheel would look like now! The curriculum is stuffed to the gills with skills to master and vocabulary to understand, recall and implement. Without regularly revisiting these themes, it is incredibly tricky to remember it all. Unfortunately, there is simply not enough time to revisit themes/topics/processes as often as is necessary to secure the children's understanding. Think back to your secondary school exams. You had to revise what you had been taught. If you didn't, chances are, you didn't do very well! The majority of us mere mortals have to revise – some of us more than others.

---

[*] Aristotle

READ WITH YOUR CHILD

The following list is what is EXPECTED of a year 6 writer:

Use prefixes and suffixes and understand the guidance for adding them	Continue to distinguish between homophones and other words which are often confused	Use knowledge of morphology and etymology in spelling and understand that the spelling of some words needs to be learnt specifically	Identify the audience and purpose for writing, selecting the appropriate form and using other similar writing as models for their own
Use dictionaries to check the spelling and meaning of words	Use a thesaurus	Write legibly, fluently and with increasing speed	Develop initial ideas, drawing on reading and research where necessary
In writing narratives, consider how authors have developed characters and settings in what pupils have read, listened to or seen performed	Select appropriate grammar and vocabulary, understanding how such choices can change and enhance meaning	In narratives, describe settings, characters and atmosphere and integrate dialogue to convey character and advance the action	Précis longer passages
Use a wide range of devices to build cohesion within and across paragraphs	Use further organisational and presentational devices to structure text and to guide the reader (for example, headings, bullet points, underlining)	Assess the effectiveness of their own and others' writing	Propose changes to vocabulary, grammar and punctuation to enhance effects and clarify meaning
Ensure the consistent and correct use of tense throughout a piece of writing	Ensure correct subject and verb agreement when using singular and plural, distinguishing between the language of speech and writing and choosing the appropriate register	Proof-read for spelling and punctuation errors	Perform their own compositions, using appropriate intonation, volume, and movement so that meaning is clear
Recognise vocabulary and structures that are appropriate for formal speech and writing, including subjunctive forms	Use passive voice to affect the presentation of information in a sentence	Use the perfect form of verbs to mark relationships of time and cause	Use expanded noun phrases to convey complicated information concisely
Use modal verbs or adverbs to indicate degrees of possibility	Use relative clauses beginning with who, which, where, when, whose, that	Use commas to clarify meaning or avoid ambiguity in writing	Use hyphens to avoid ambiguity
Use brackets, dashes or commas to indicate parenthesis	Use semi-colons, colons or dashes to mark boundaries between independent clauses	Use a colon to introduce a list	Punctuating bullet points consistently

Remember, that's just writing! If you feel overwhelmed and like giving up, imagine how your average ten-year-old is feeling! Now consider reading and comprehension, maths, science and everything else... To be absolutely clear, that list is what is needed to reach A.R.E (age-related expectations) it is not greater depth/achieving beyond what is expected.

To best help our children, I believe a cultural shift is needed. Parents need to start building slightly more sophisticated language into their lives at home if our children are to have the best chance of achieving what is expected of them, without becoming horribly stressed and anxious. Let's consider Ebbinghaus' Forgetting Curve[*]:

Ebbinghaus Curve of Forgetting

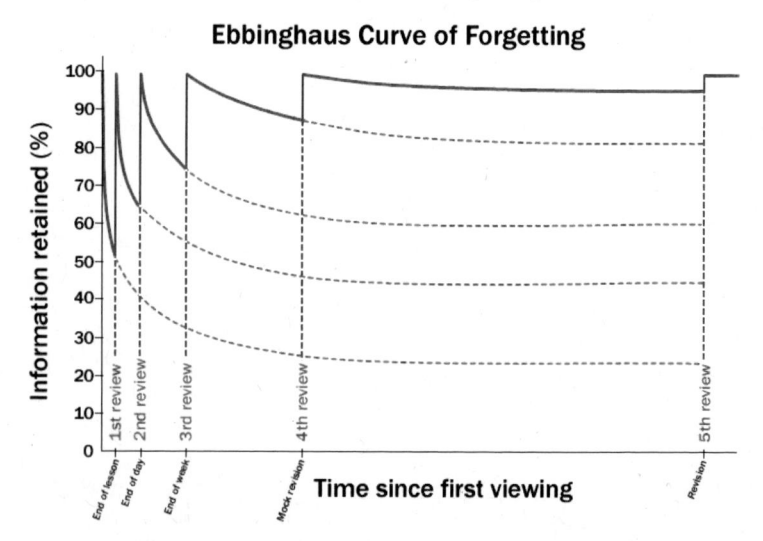

Illustration from: *The Rules of Revision*, Liam Porritt.
https://liamporritt.com

---

[*] Hermann Ebbinghaus PhD, 1850 - 1909

By revisiting concepts frequently, we far are less likely to forget them. Common sense, I know, but it's always good to have a bit of science on your side as back up. I took the illustration of the curve from Liam Porritt's book *The Rules of Revision*. As your children get older and face secondary school challenges, I highly recommend you look to Liam for help and guidance.

Spend your time with your child wisely. Talking to them about how ridiculous you think the system is will not help them. Moaning about the educational policy will not help them reach their potential – it will only serve to demotivate and give them excuses. Write letters to those in power if you feel passionately enough, go on a protest rally or create a petition by all means, BUT make sure you plough an equal amount of energy into positive steps to support your child because they are living in the here and now. Be positive and playful. Rise to the challenge – teach yourself something new…grow together and achieve together.

Child's play
It may seem overwhelming, but it needn't be. The whole process can be achieved by playing games in the car or on the walk to school. It can be seamlessly built into the bedtime routine and story-time. Mealtimes, at home or out and about, provide the perfect opportunity for light-hearted, fun, family learning which will enrich your relationship with your child, enable them at school (relieving stress and anxiety) and ensure they reach their potential. Flo and I spoke about adverbs[*] when I was plaiting her hair a

---

[*] If in doubt, get the vocabulary list out ☺

few days ago – it came up naturally…something about me pulling too tightly! Sound familiar? It came up 'naturally' because I've practised. A few years ago, it would have felt a bit odd, but now it's part of our lives. That was probably the only thing 'school' related I mentioned that day… I'm not grilling my child. Flo asks to play my games regularly because she loves my undivided attention. The games make me engage with her…the fact they are loaded with opportunities to improve her speaking and listening skills is a happy accident. I'm not the 'perfect mother' by any stretch of the imagination. Right now, it's gone noon, Flo is still in her pyjamas, she's had terrible cereal for breakfast and she's watching television. It's the school holidays – I figure, why not? Some may judge that as positively dreadful parenting. Luckily for me, my hard-won, long-fought parenting force-field means I can deflect their opinions and continue tapping away at my laptop!

I don't put an 'age limit' on the games we have played. Florence has been playing most of them since she was about four years old.

> If a toddler can learn about a 'tyrannosaurus-rex' a four-year-old can learn about 'alliteration'.
>
> **STAFFROOM SECRET**

It's our attitude or fear that often puts artificial limits on our children's learning. Take logical steps and introduce something new when you feel they are ready. You're the best judge of that – you know them best. When children are toddlers, we sing with them, read to them, play I-spy, and chit-chat about the world around us. Why do we stop? All that chit-chat was learning. As parents, we start as brilliant teachers but tend to resign from the post too early. Happily, however, we clearly know how to do it. Now, all we need to do is keep going... We need to keep up the chit-chat, songs and games – they simply need to change a little as our children grow.

@staffroom_secrets

I have an Instagram account that I regularly update with games to be played on the school run, whether you walk or go in the car. Flo knows them so well she plays them with friends on the playground and on long coach journeys (school trip fun). If you have an account, it's a handy tool to have in your pocket. We play whilst I cook diner or wait at Pizza Express (other Italian restaurants are available) for our meals to be prepared. The whole family can get involved or you can play as a pair.

IRONIC
The song that contains no irony

Knowing how to classify the language we use is part and parcel of primary school life, whether we like it or not. Word classes: nouns (there are a few of those), verbs, adjectives, adverbs, are just the start. Prepositions and determiners puzzle pupils across the nation; metaphors and similes are constantly confused; conjunctions (be they coordinating or subordinate) baffle our young learners; subordinate/relative/embedded and main clauses are tricky to spot; passive and active voice would be best taught by Yoda; and personification is enough to make even the sun sigh in resignation and refuse to shine. If you were lucky enough to be taught all of this, trust me, you are in the minority! For the rest of us, let's not panic – there's a vocabulary list in the back.

It's a lot to take on board. Little wonder children get anxious... By playing a few games at home and using some of the language children are required to be familiar with, you would be covertly revising with your child and lowering their class-based anxiety. Moreover, you'll be demonstrating to your child that you are invested and involved in their world – showing them that what they do at school interests and matters to you.

Speaking and listening

A surprising number of children (in year 6 and beyond) are struggling to speak in coherent, fluent, confident sentences. By playing these verbal games with your children, you'll be working on these key skills, which (to the surprise of many, who believe it will just 'develop naturally') need to be explicitly practised in order to be mastered.

I'm thinking of a…

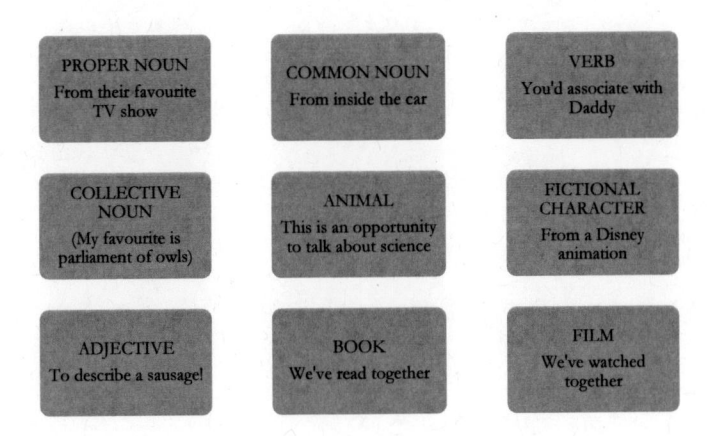

PROPER NOUN From their favourite TV show	COMMON NOUN From inside the car	VERB You'd associate with Daddy
COLLECTIVE NOUN (My favourite is parliament of owls)	ANIMAL This is an opportunity to talk about science	FICTIONAL CHARACTER From a Disney animation
ADJECTIVE To describe a sausage!	BOOK We've read together	FILM We've watched together

These are just a few examples. I'm sure you get the idea and could develop and expand on the general theme…

In these games, players ask yes/no style questions to eventually get to the answer. For the proper noun, you'd start by asking, 'Is it a person?' or, 'Is it a place?' perhaps, 'Is it a thing?' What's key here is using the correct language – that's the power of these games; it's all about creating opportunities for your children to hear the language and contextualise it. Before long, they'll be comfortable using this language and applying it; they'll start spotting adjectives in adverts on telly or verbs in their reading. The other beauty of these games is that they create opportunities to talk descriptively. Confident, descriptive writing is born out of confident, descriptive speaking. This is especially true if your child is a reluctant reader – they need to be exposed to language and enrich their vocabulary through the power of a good natter. Because, as a family, we have played these games so much, Flo has really benefited. When playing **I'm thinking of an animal**, she'll ask questions like: is it an omnivore, is it canine, is it feline, is it a mammal…? She's not 'clever'; she's simply copying what she's learned from her big sisters and John and me. It's been a natural, easy, FUN process. My favourite memory of this game was from a pizza night, whilst we were on holiday. Her animal turned out to be a head louse! It took us ages to get, and we ended up crying with laughter. I hoped none of the other diners spoke English!

Tell me more!

This is a version of 'I went to the shops, and I bought…' which is a memory game. I came up with this one because children in Year 2 have to know what an expanded noun phrase is and they have to use them. As children work their way through primary school, we expect them to write more and more complex sentences. This game works on the skills required to do just that.

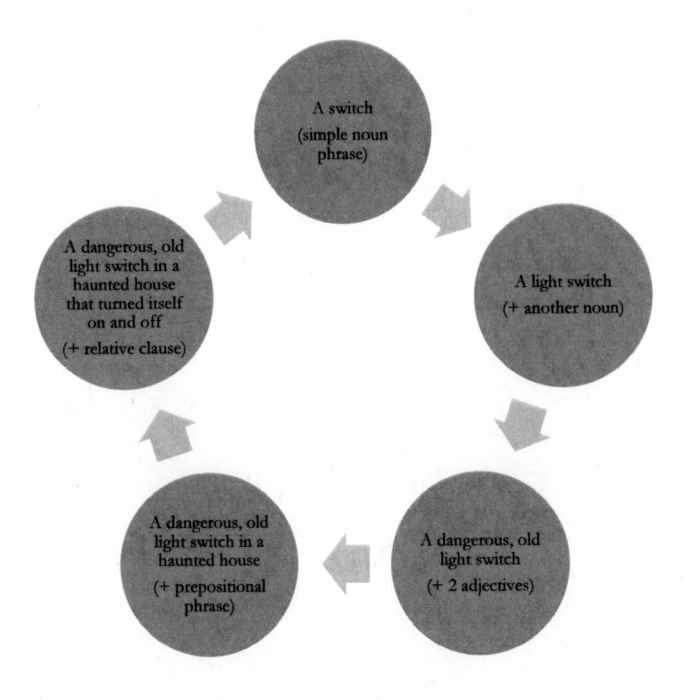

- A switch (simple noun phrase)
- A light switch (+ another noun)
- A dangerous, old light switch (+ 2 adjectives)
- A dangerous, old light switch in a haunted house (+ prepositional phrase)
- A dangerous, old light switch in a haunted house that turned itself on and off (+ relative clause)

Children in my year 5 class are expected to know all that. For children in year 2, the expanded noun phrase: *a dangerous, old switch* would suffice.

The alliteration game:

As mentioned earlier, we play the alliteration game in the car. We work alphabetically and take turns: Animated Ant, Barbequing Buffalo, etc… Bonus points for 3 or 4 worders: Dangerously drunken, delirious dinosaur! Make sure you use the correct language. Declare with a fanfare and a silly, dramatic voice. "It's time for the

ALLITERATION game, and here's your host, Uncle Simon!"

Are you old enough to remember Mallet's Mallet?

It was a word association game, where an initial word was offered for you to associate with. If, for example, it started with the word 'jelly' a suitable response would be 'custard', followed perhaps by 'pudding' and then 'meals' and so on… If you paused for too long (or repeated something), you got hit on the head with a foam mallet, wielded by an excitable, bespectacled chap wearing a shell-suit. The same principle (mallets, spectacles and shell-suits optional) can be employed in this next game.

Flo and I sing and clap this to start:

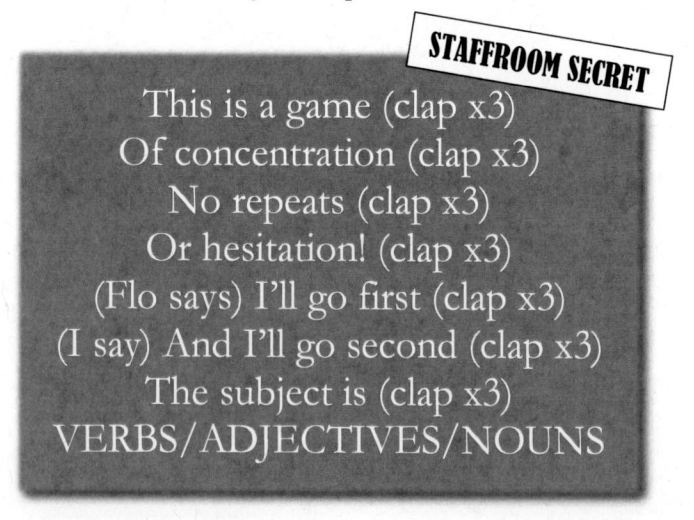

STAFFROOM SECRET

This is a game (clap x3)
Of concentration (clap x3)
No repeats (clap x3)
Or hesitation! (clap x3)
(Flo says) I'll go first (clap x3)
(I say) And I'll go second (clap x3)
The subject is (clap x3)
VERBS/ADJECTIVES/NOUNS

Top tip: pat your thighs twice when you say the words to the song, then add the claps (pat, pat, clap, clap, clap). The challenge is to keep the rhythm going! Each person has to say a word in time to the two pats on the thighs. You've then got 3 claps before the next person says their word. You can play with all the word classes...use the vocabulary list in the back of the book for inspiration. Flo and I played this at the shops recently whilst Lottie was trying on some clothes. If the subject is, for example, ADJECTIVE, I'll usually assign a noun to it, e.g. "ADJECTIVE to describe NANNY."

You can employ the same rules to synonyms and antonyms[*]. Cut the children some slack on time when they start but be tough on the adults! 'Said' is a great one for synonyms: said, uttered, mumbled, declared, announced, yelled, muttered, whispered, spluttered, cried… DO NOT AVOID THESE GAMES IF YOU ARE NOT VERY GOOD AT THEM. Your children need to see you struggle. You can look up words together and be sure to create opportunities to use them again.

Happy homophones

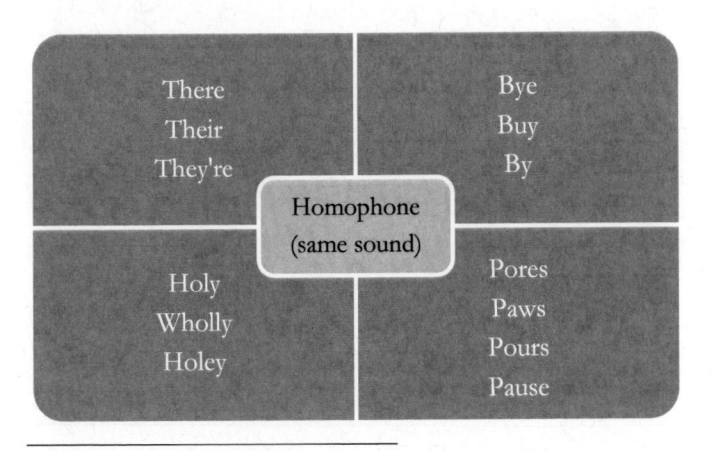

There Their They're	Bye Buy By
Holy Wholly Holey	Pores Paws Pours Pause

Homophone (same sound)

---

[*] Synonym: similar word. Antonym: word of opposite meaning

When children are little, start by explaining what a homophone is: words that sound the same but have different meanings (homo: same, phone: sound) and give a few examples.

Later in the day get them to tell someone else what a homophone is. If they don't remember, which they probably won't, remind them. Make it fun! Pea is a fun one. Pea and pee are entirely different! A quick google will arm you with plenty, then you can play around with putting them into funny sentences. Before long, your little one (not won) will be spotting homophones all over the place (not plaice) and challenging you to make up silly sentences. Challenge them to think of some homophones on a car journey – you should play too (to, two, tutu). See (sea) if their (there, they're) ideas are better than yours! They can keep score to see who thinks of the most.

> The holy man wore a holey jumper, which was wholly useless in the freezing church.

STAFFROOM SECRET

FIGURE it out:
This game explores FIGURATIVE language, which is anything that is NOT LITERAL. Beth and Lottie never really had an issue with this, but Flo continues to struggle and needs figurative speech to be explained. If I say, "I'll be 2 minutes" she now understands that is a figure of speech – it is not literal, and she should not start counting! As mad as a hatter, daft as a brush, quick as a flash, sweet as

pie – all these, and many more, are often phrases we take for granted, but many children need them to be explained. It's important that when we do this, we use the correct language. Simile, metaphor, personification and idioms are all forms of FIGURATIVE language, and our children are expected to know the difference between them all.

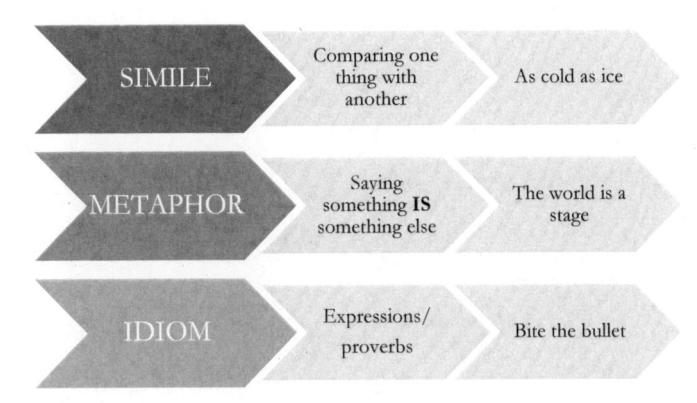

SIMILE	Comparing one thing with another	As cold as ice
METAPHOR	Saying something **IS** something else	The world is a stage
IDIOM	Expressions/proverbs	Bite the bullet

A quick search online will throw up a mountain of these, so keep 'em peeled and don't let the side down! Once you have got some ideas, you can play. Here are a few examples:

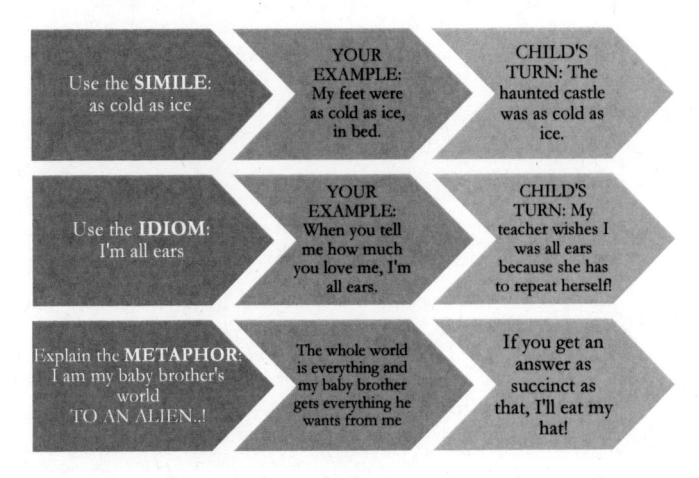

Use the **SIMILE**: as cold as ice	YOUR EXAMPLE: My feet were as cold as ice, in bed.	CHILD'S TURN: The haunted castle was as cold as ice.
Use the **IDIOM**: I'm all ears	YOUR EXAMPLE: When you tell me how much you love me, I'm all ears.	CHILD'S TURN: My teacher wishes I was all ears because she has to repeat herself!
Explain the **METAPHOR**: I am my baby brother's world TO AN ALIEN..!	The whole world is everything and my baby brother gets everything he wants from me	If you get an answer as succinct as that, I'll eat my hat!

You could extend the game to include **personification**, where non-human things are given human characteristics.

Personification puzzles

Challenge your child to spot the personification AND explain it.

- New York – the city that never sleeps!
- The flower was screaming out for water.
- The stars were winking in the night sky.

Challenge them to come up with some examples of their own.

Becoming confident with these concepts really enhances a child's writing and (perhaps even more crucially) their comprehension of reading.

Clean up with this mnemonic*

One of Lottie and Florence's favourite tools for writing good stories is **SHAMPOO**. Tell your child all about SHAMPOO, and they too will feel super-confident in the classroom. The girls challenge themselves to use as much SHAMPOO as possible in their writing because they know good SHAMPOO creates interesting reading (it also ticks superheroes' boxes).

---

a system which assists in remembering something

Simile
Hyperbole
Alliteration
Metaphor
Personification
Onomatopoeia
Oxymoron (seriously funny/act naturally/sweet sorrow – contradictory word pairs)

The oxymoron is an extra challenge – it's just a bit of fun to try and spot them or use one if the writing allows. It's not a curriculum requirement.

What on earth is a fronted adverbial phrase?!

When I first started working at Culverstone School, I worked in Year 5 as a 1:1. In one of the first lessons I attended, the teacher started talking gobble-de-gook! I couldn't grasp what she was going on about, and it was nothing to do with her fabulous Irish accent! The worry was, some of the children seemed to be nodding along and contributing ideas. I was in trouble. How was I going to support this glorious child with a task I had no clue about? My pulse was racing; I could feel myself going red. I had to put my hand up. "I'm so sorry Miss Donovan, but what is a fronted adverbial phrase?" A reassuring smile calmed my blushes.

"That is a really good question. To be honest, Mrs Chappell, I think a fair few of us in here are still struggling with it! Right, who's going to explain it…?"

Fronted adverbials/adverbial phrases

Put simply, these go at the **beginning** of a sentence to give **more detail** about what's happening. They **add** to the **verb** that is about to follow. **Adverbs** tell us HOW, WHEN, WHERE, WHY and HOW LONG things happen. A fronted adverbial is a **single** word: eventually, suddenly, miraculously, etc. followed by an action: she **dived** into the pool/he **professed** his love/they **spoke** to each another… A fronted adverbial phrase is a collection of words to **add** to the upcoming **verb:** On Tuesday afternoon/ After an hour of agony/ Despite the advice…followed by the action: she **approached** the judge/she **left** the room/she **screamed** at the police officer. The **fronted** adverbial or adverbial phrase is always followed by a **comma**.

Adverb Adventures

In this game, I offer up a simple sentence: *The man walked to work,* and I challenge the children to think of three contrasting fronted adverbials/adverbial phrases to put before their readers to explain how the verb is performed. Depending on their age/experience, they might offer:

- Quickly,
- Without a care,
- After his extraordinarily indulgent breakfast,

I encourage the children to emphasise the comma with a karate chop action because I want them to remember their all-important punctuation.

The importance of oracy

Oracy is the ability to articulate ideas, develop understanding and engage with others through spoken language*. The development of oracy involves physical, linguistic, cognitive, and social and emotional processes. Opportunities to speak and actively listen are vital to a child's development. As well as playing the verbal games I have set out in this chapter, remember to chat with your child about the world in which they live – ask them questions, ask for their opinion, and encourage them to 'tell you more…' Here are some ideas to get you started:

- What do you daydream about?
- What sounds make you happy?
- What would you like to do all by yourself?
- If you ran a restaurant, what would it be like?
- What would you write a book about?

Take it easy

The key to all this is **fun**. Do not get frustrated. Some adults become infuriated if children forget something they have done with them, or take a while to grasp a concept. Trust me – the child will pick up on that in a flash. Bam! There's your label. It doesn't matter if you resist saying something out loud – they'll read your body language and pick up on your negativity. Suddenly, you have a sad/embarrassed/angry/demotivated/humiliated young person on your hands. Consequently, fight/flight/freeze comes into play, and, inevitably, they will struggle to learn… Trust is a huge part of creating the right environment in

---

* https://voice21.org/oracy/

which to learn. The Montessori goddesses and Lottie's English superhero both earned their children's trust. Children must feel safe to fail. The learning that takes place through playing these games takes YEARS – not hours to master. Realistic expectations are essential. Start playing the games as part of your daily routine. Not all of them at once! They will pre-teach and/or consolidate learning. They will boost your child's confidence and lower anxiety in the classroom, which will in turn facilitate more learning.

If this chapter has made your stomach sink because you are feeling overwhelmed by the language you are unfamiliar with, please do not give up. The feeling you are experiencing is exactly what many of the children in school experience. Read the chapter again. Look at the vocabulary in the back. Take it step by step. One game at a time. You will get there. I didn't know the majority of this 'stuff' a few years ago, but I persevered – you owe it to your children to do the same. Don't give in to fear – you've got this. It bears repeating…

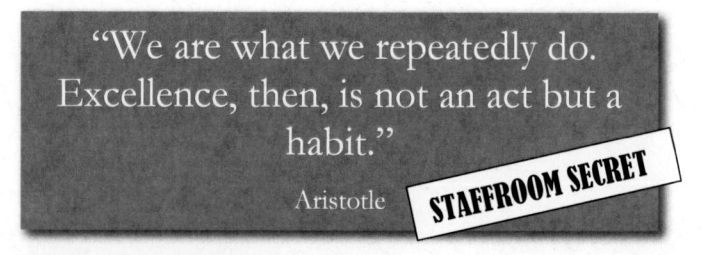

> "We are what we repeatedly do. Excellence, then, is not an act but a habit."
> Aristotle

STAFFROOM SECRET

I'll be honest Aristotle, excellence doesn't really interest me, but truly UNDERSTANDING something really 'floats my boat'!

KNOCK THREE TIMES

Not your head on a brick wall – that won't help at all…

My relationship with maths has been complicated: it was not love at first sight. It's difficult to recall when the misunderstandings between us started, but I suspect I was about seven years old. Looking back, my life was rich with language: chit-chat, songs, stories, television… I absorbed the English language and inadvertently became comfortable in its company – I understood many of its facets. Maths and I, however, met comparatively rarely: once every weekday for about an hour. Our relationship was not invested in – our common ground was not illuminated, celebrated or sufficiently explored because it was not part of my everyday life, and my mum was scared of it. For a long time, Maths and I were estranged. I faked loving Maths for the sake of Beth's education. As a result, we got closer; now, we're friends.

Maths is all around us; we have to make a conscious effort to highlight its beauty to our children and celebrate its fun-side! Play cards and board games to explore counting and patterns; cook together and talk about the weights and measures – be sure to estimate and talk about equivalents (grams and ounces, pounds and kilograms); have a height chart against the door but let the children do the measuring; let them sum the total of a small shop and let them pay in cash – count aloud as the change is given. Compare things: tallest, smallest, longest, shortest, fastest, most expensive…

I have many, many parents banging their heads against brick walls when it comes to maths. Word problems are usually the beauties that get the eyes rolling and the heart racing. The reason (partly) is because, historically, we have separated maths from language. If you teach pages of abstract equations without context, it's hardly surprising children find it difficult to implement the operations they have learned. Language should be at the heart of mathematics. You can't master a skill if you do not deeply understand it. We need to *talk* about numbers. Here are some games to try:

I'm thinking of a number …

- 0 to 20
- 0 to 100
- 0 to 1,000…

In these games, players ask yes/no style questions to eventually get to the answer. Questions asked should include some of the following:

READ WITH YOUR CHILD

Is it **odd**?	Is the **digit** in the 'ones column' less than 6?	Is it **between** 10 and 20?	Can it be **equally divided** into two **parts**?
Is it **less than** 50?	Is it a **multiple** of 5?	Is it **even**?	Is it a **3-digit** number?
Is the **digit** in the **'tens column' greater** than 5?	Is it a **2-digit** number?	Is it **greater/more** than 50?	Is it in my 7 **times-tables**?

You get the idea. It's all about language and the power of using it. Some of the examples have more sophisticated language than others; gradually introduce this once your child is secure with the simpler concepts. By hearing the language, children begin to contextualise it and then (before we know it) they start using it too. Play as a pair to start off with – you should **work with your child** to answer the questions **someone else** is asking. By working as a pair, you'll be able to master *thinking out loud*. Children need to hear the mental processes and (whenever possible) see them too.

That's odd!

When you begin to tackle odd and even numbers, you could draw, use building blocks or even Cheerios/Smarties etc. to illustrate the point and build your child's confidence. They'll do something similar at school, of course, but this chance to re-visit or pre-learn will be most welcomed by your little (or not so little) learner.

READ WITH YOUR CHILD

ODD and EVEN numbers should be delicious!

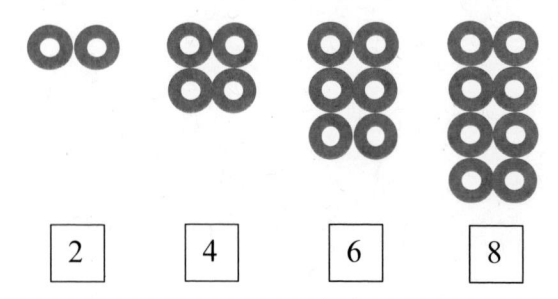

| 2 | 4 | 6 | 8 |

Notice how each Cheerio/Smartie has a 'friend' alongside? That's how we can **see** they are EVEN numbers. If your child does not know if a number is odd or even, draw it, make it out of Cheerios/Smarties or count in groups of 2. Help them **discover** that the even numbers will always end in either 0,2,4,6 or 8 and then explain that is a 'rule'.

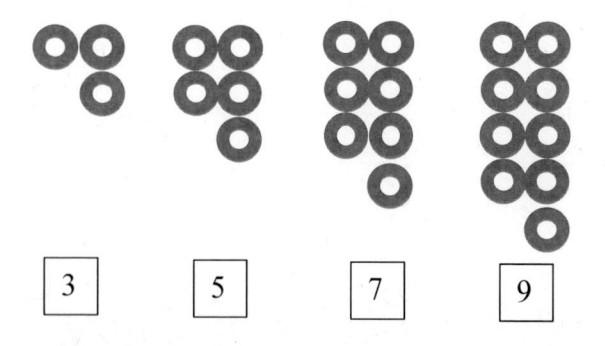

| 3 | 5 | 7 | 9 |

Notice how there is always a Cheerio/Smartie without a friend? That's how we can **see** they are ODD numbers. Help them **discover** that the ODD numbers will always end in either 1,3,5,7 or 9 and then explain that is a 'rule'.

Once the children are confident with the rule, you can have fun by writing huge numbers and 'impressing' friends and family when they can identify the given number as either odd or even (just by looking at the last digit).

Give Me 5 or Give Me 10:

In this game, you challenge children to give you 5 facts about a number. As players become more competent, you challenge them to give you 10 facts. Let's say the number is 10.

10 is an even number, I know this because it ends in a zero	10 is a 2-digit number	The 1 represents one lot of ten because it is in the tens-column	The zero represents no lots of one because it is in the ones-column	My age is 4 lots of 10 add half of ten!
10 is double 5 because 5 add 5 is ten or 2 lots of 5 is equivalent to 10	10 is half of twenty because 20 shared between 2 is 10	10 squared is 100 because 10 multiplied by itself (10) is 100	The third multiple of 10 is 30: First: 10 Second: 20 Third: 30	Factor pairs of 10 are 1&10 and 2&5. I know this because 1x10 =10 and 2x5=10

You'll need to 'model' this at first – working with your child – verbalising your thought process. Always try to justify your answer – we ask the children to do this in school, so it will be good to practise. Using correct and varied language is so important because it gives our children exposure to the tools they need to master mathematical concepts.

Here are a few extra pointers:
- **Addition:** sum, add, altogether, total, increase, plus
- **Subtraction:** subtract, take away, less, difference, decrease, fewer
- **Multiplication:** multiply, times, lots of, groups of, repeated addition, product
- **Division:** divide, divided by, divided into, shared, equally split, group into
- **Equals:** makes, same as, total, balances, equivalent

If children struggle with the notion of all these different ways of expressing the same thing, remind them of all the words they use to express things in English (synonyms). Happy: gleeful, jolly, merry, ecstatic, pleased… The more language we can use, the better. Top tip: **SUM** means to add, so do not use it generically when talking about mathematical equations. A page of multiplication acknowledged with the comment 'great sums' is not helpful!

Helpful manipulatives

Manipulatives are objects designed to help learners perceive a concept by holding it and manipulating it – hence the name. Although you can use things around the house (building bricks, stock cubes, breakfast cereal…), you may want to invest in some specific materials. Toy money is brilliant! I use it all the time, and I have even made a £1,000 note from a 'tweaked' *Twinkl* resource. Twinkl have cut-out notes and coins which you could use if you don't want plastic ones. I love my fraction tower that shows equivalents (decimals, percentages), and my place value counters have been helpful.

Rhymes Times-tables

The first one Flo and I made up together was:

3, 6, 9 monkeys in a line
12, 15, 18 monkeys bored of waiting
21 monkeys having fun
24 dancing through the door
27 monkeys up in heaven
30, 33, 36 clever sticks!

By creating this together, Flo went over and over the numbers. We used funny voices and made up actions to get the body involved and build more neural pathways. Flo drew pictures (including the numbers), and we spoke about REPEATED ADDITION and MULTIPLES. Now I can say, 'give me a multiple of 3 Flo' and she'll say '21' (for example), then she might add, 'That's a multiple of 7 too mummy.' That's because we've learned all the tables in the same way, so she's built relationships between the numbers. It's been a slow, steady, fun-filled journey, full of verbal, visual, physical and logical learning. It is often repeated in the car or in the playground (it's like a clapping game, so it's fun to share). The times-tables are hard to learn – especially if you are not a logical, linear learner. Flo and I still practise them now. She started the journey aged about 4. If we don't practise regularly, we forget them or become rusty. For most of us, it's a case of – if you don't use it, you lose it. As Flo has got older, she's been able to drop the rhyme and simply recall the facts. She is beginning to know (without thinking) many of her multiplications. Don't feel embarrassed if you don't remember your times-tables. Learn them with your child. Get those fingers out and let them see you adding on. In fact, if you do know them, there's a lot to be said for *pretending* you don't. There's nothing quite as memorable as learning something new with a person you love. I am not a linear learner; I have all sorts of wacky stuff going on in my head to recall times-table facts: Vix and Stephan went to the zoo, 6 x 7 is 42! I am like, in my experience, lots of people... There are always children (linear learners) in my class who can complete a times-table square quicker than I can. I think that's wonderful. It isn't something I shy away from sharing. I have great fun trying to beat them! We celebrate our different brains, laugh at my competitiveness, and I use it as a great excuse to get children to 'help me' by coming up with strategies to improve my results. Once everyone's effort is recognised, I'll challenge my linear learners with the 13 times-table and a host of division questions.

Factors

You can build on the times-tables knowledge by introducing FACTORS. Factors bamboozle my Year 5 children with dreadful, predictable regularity. It's because they are not used to the language. Factors are the numbers that can be multiplied to make a given number. I find these are best seen by looking at a FACTOR BUG*. May I heartily suggest you get creative and make some of these. My class made some wonderful bugs for home-learning. We had springing legs, pipe-cleaners, paper plates and even a full-on costume complete with peek-a-boo flaps and hinges*!

---

* A superhero named Phil Jack taught me about factor bugs. Phil Jack knows so much stuff! To his own admission, most of it is useless but factor bugs are great ☺

* Big up Daisy & family. x

READ WITH YOUR CHILD

The 'given' number is in the nose! So, our 'given' number is 32. The FACTORS of 32 are displayed around the outside of the bug. ALWAYS start with 1 on the left. Then ask, "What multiplied by 1 makes (in this case) 32?" The answer to that question goes on the opposite side. Work chronologically through the numbers until there are no more options. In this example the number 3 was not needed, BUT make sure the child checks to make sure – don't do it for them! By the end of the game, we can see the FACTORS of 32 are: 1,2,4,8,16 and 32 by reading around the bug, anti-clockwise.

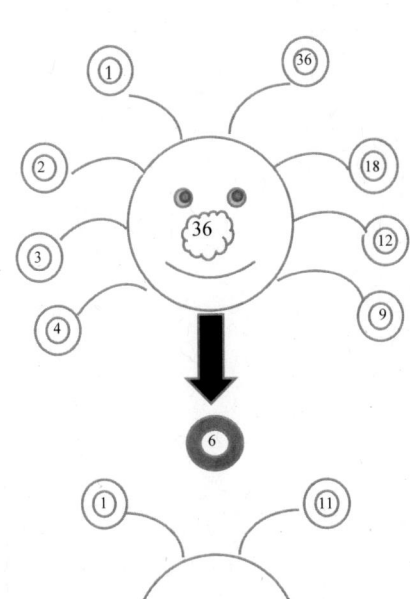

In this example, our 'given' number is 36. Notice its **tail**! The tail proves that we have discovered a SQUARE number, which is very exciting when you are about 7-years-old! To introduce more rich language, you could say (and encourage your children to say) "The **product** of 3 and 12 is 36."

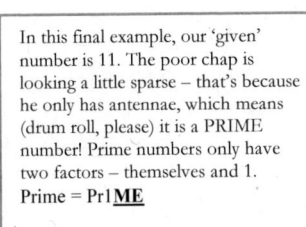

In this final example, our 'given' number is 11. The poor chap is looking a little sparse – that's because he only has antennae, which means (drum roll, please) it is a PRIME number! Prime numbers only have two factors – themselves and 1.
Prime = Pr1**ME**

READ WITH YOUR CHILD

Build me up

To further explore square numbers, why not build the square? You could use building blocks, stock cubes, cereal or chocolate chunks. The square of 4 is calculated by multiplying 4 by itself: 4x4 = 16. To prove it is a 'square number' build it! It works for cubed numbers too, but you can quickly run out of building blocks!

This has created a **square** array to illustrate that 4x4=16

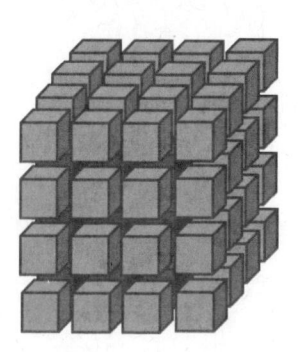

This has created a **cube** to illustrate that 4 **cubed** is 64 because it shows that 4x4=16, which when multiplied by 4 for a **third** time = 64

In my daughter's Montessori school, mathematical concepts were always introduced with solid objects to help children contextualise. When I first started teaching in primary school, I was horrified to see this was not the case. Of late however, there has been somewhat of a transformation in our classrooms with MANIPULATIVES being introduced to help children understand concepts and solve equations. It has been heralded in many schools as a revolutionary new approach! New?! Please…

Number Family Fortunes

In this game, we encourage children to ask, 'If I've calculated this fact, what other facts do I know?' Blocks can be used in arrays to show the relationship between division and multiplication. These relationships are often referred to in school as number families.

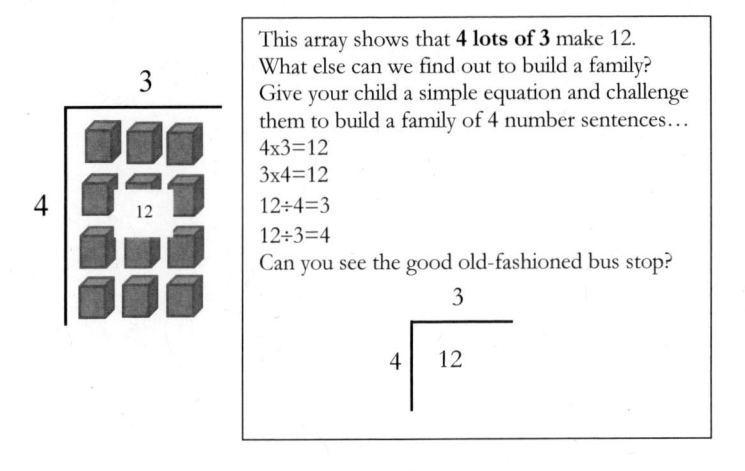

> This array shows that **4 lots of 3** make 12.
> What else can we find out to build a family?
> Give your child a simple equation and challenge them to build a family of 4 number sentences…
> 4x3=12
> 3x4=12
> 12÷4=3
> 12÷3=4
> Can you see the good old-fashioned bus stop?

Encourage your child to physically 'perform' the equations. If they are hesitant, show them a few times, then do it together. They will eventually want to work independently – it's how they are designed.

Number bonds

Number bonds are simply the pairs of numbers that make up a given number. 'Families' can be built when children apply their knowledge of these bonds. Give your child an equation which includes a number bond they are familiar with, then work with them to find the rest of the family. Once you've done it with them a few times, they'll be able to do it independently. This is great for building strong mathematical neural pathways in your child's brain.

10 = 6 + 4

If you know that, what else do you know? Let's build a number family... Use blocks/cereal and encourage your children to physically prove their equations.

10 = 6 + 4
10 = 4 + 6
6 = 10 – 4
4 = 10 – 6

Notice how I put the equals sign on the other side of the equation? It's important to do that in order to deepen their understanding of what = really means. Number families introduce *inverse operations*. In maths, add and subtract are the inverse of one another, just as multiply and divide are: one reverses the effect of the other. Children need to be comfortable with this concept and use inverse operations to support their initial calculations.

Shapeshifters

This game is great for car journeys but be warned – once you start playing it, you'll never look at the world in the same way again. You simply have to spot shapes. Once you've given one example of a shape (let's say rectangle – window) you can't use window again but keep looking to increase your total. To add a challenge, start hunting down 3D shapes. Children start finding shapes everywhere: car-stickers, the ornaments people dangle from their rear-view mirrors, buildings and monuments. I find it highly addictive and inadvertently find myself playing when no one else is in the car. Last week, I got overly excited and shouted, 'Sphere!' when I spotted a dandelion-seed-head. I know – tragic. Once everyone is confident with identifying shapes, start introducing the language to describe their properties. Keep it playful. Pretend you don't know things: suddenly remember the underside of the lorry and add another 'face' to your total. I tend to get the children to time a minute and see how many they can find in that magical 60 seconds. One thing is for certain, on our roads, there are always plenty of cones to be found! If you spot a pyramid: 1,000 bonus points (unless you are on holiday in Egypt).

Helpful language:

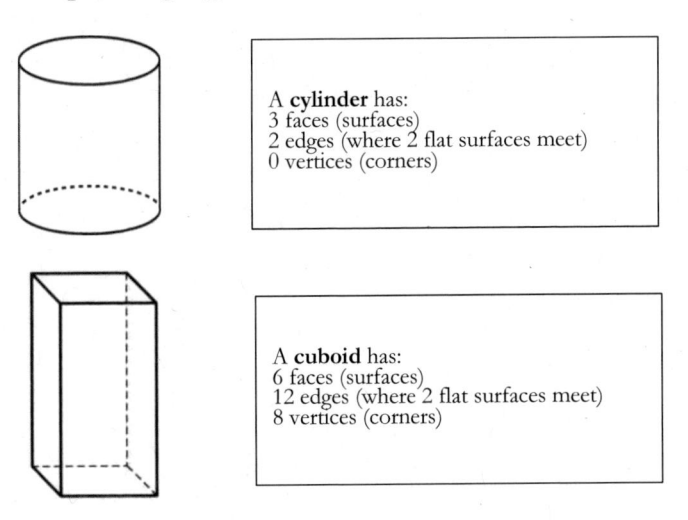

A **cylinder** has:
3 faces (surfaces)
2 edges (where 2 flat surfaces meet)
0 vertices (corners)

A **cuboid** has:
6 faces (surfaces)
12 edges (where 2 flat surfaces meet)
8 vertices (corners)

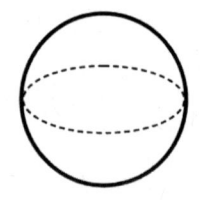

A **sphere** has:
1 face (surface)
0 edges (where 2 flat surfaces meet)
0 vertices (corners)

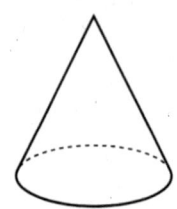

A **cone** has:
2 faces (surfaces)
1 edge (where 2 flat surfaces meet)
0 vertices (corners)

Sugar and spice and all things nice:

Usually, I'd argue that sugar is bad for children, but when it's in those little, long, thin sachets I love it! I'll give Flo 5 and say, 'Make me a pentagon'. Or I'll give her six and ask, 'What shape can you make with that?' I might ask her how many she'll need for a heptagon… It's one of her favourite things to do in a café. Of course, you are not limited to sugar sachets. You could use pencils, cocktail sticks, toothpicks… To jog your memory:

5 = pentagon
6 = hexagon
7 = heptagon
8 = octagon
9 = nonagon
10 = decagon

There's more than one way to skin a banana!

I'm going to give one example of how things can be done differently to the 'formal column' method most of us are used to. Once children know the options, they can choose which method they prefer. Resist the urge to scoff a method other than the one you are comfortable with. Model curiosity, take a healthy interest, ask your child to teach you something…you might prefer another method if you have an open mind and give it a go. Let's look at multiplication using **partitioning** or the **grid/box** method: 42 x32

x	40	2
30	**1200**	**60**
2	**80**	**4**

This method 'partitions' the numbers to highlight their place value. We can see that 42 is made up of 40 and 2, so that's 4 lots of ten and 2 ones. To complete the grid the children are told to momentarily disregard the zeros, so the metal maths is simplified. E.g. 3x4 = 12. Once they have calculated the 12 they must re-introduce the zeros to move the digits back to the correct place value. As 2 zeros had been 'removed', 2 zeros must be put back to give us the true answer of 1,200. The same process is repeated for each box. Once all the multiplication of the tens and ones is complete, the children sum their boxes to reach the answer.

1,200 + 80 + 60 + 4 = **1,344**

Many children prefer this method because they do not need to 'carry' and the place value is clearer.

What is the Singapore bar everyone is talking about?

Sadly, it's not a swanky gin bar or micro-brewery. It is, however, a way of representing word problems, to help children (and adults) visualise a problem and therefore see what steps they need to take in order to solve it, which may negate the need for adults to hit the gin bar! This method works by representing parts and wholes. I taught it to Lottie recently, and she loved it – she used it in her GCSE and saved herself a heap of time and energy in the process.

A one-step question might be: Sajid and Tina have 550 marbles. Sajid has 245 marbles. **How many marbles does Tina have?**

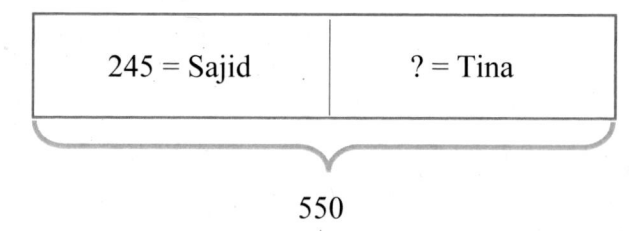

| 245 = Sajid | ? = Tina |

550

The one-step example shows how the bar represents 'the whole'. By drawing the bar, children can see they need to find the missing part to complete the 550. They can choose how they will do this. Perhaps they'll add on from 245 to reach 550, or they might prefer to subtract 245 from 550. By learning this method, much more complicated questions, with multiple steps can be represented, visualised and successfully tackled.

READ WITH YOUR CHILD

Here is a typical two-step question: Rodney has 24 marbles more than Gurpreet, who has 73 marbles. **How many marbles does Rodney have and how many marbles do they have altogether?**

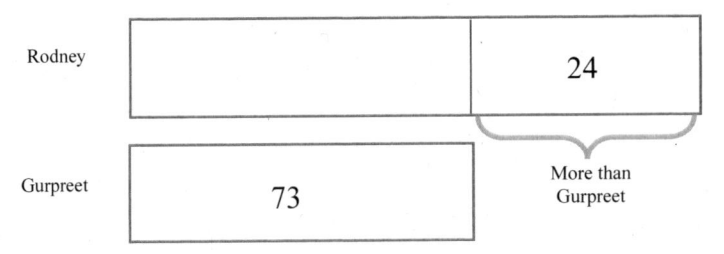

| Rodney | | 24 |

Gurpreet | 73 | More than Gurpreet

Here, we can see that to calculate Rodney's total we need to add 24 to 73. To calculate the number of marbles altogether we will need to sum Rodney and Gurpreet's bars.

> The bar method is great for helping children with their fractions
>
> **STAFFROOM SECRET**

A shop has 56 apples. $\frac{4}{7}$ of the apples are green, the others are red. **How many apples are red?**

The denominator at the bottom of the fraction (the 7) tells us how many equal parts to split our bar into.

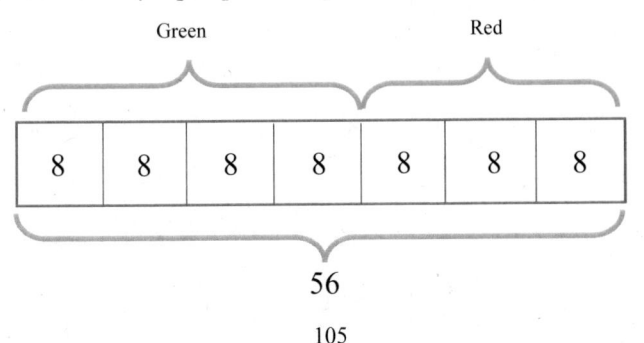

Green | Red

| 8 | 8 | 8 | 8 | 8 | 8 | 8 |

56

This example serves as a reminder of why learning the times-tables is so important. A child who knows their times-tables will recognise 56 (apples) divided into 7 equal parts and know that each part has a value of 8. They know 7x8 = 56 and so (by using the inverse or 'number family') know 56 divided by 7 is 8. A child who does not know their times-table facts will waste valuable time using trial and error to work out which number they need to fill each box. Likewise, calculating the answer is much easier for the child who knows their tables. They know that 3x8 is 24; they do not need to use repeated addition or a timely, formal column multiplication method. If your child has a specific processing issue that makes learning times-tables especially difficult, ensure they have a times-table square to refer to.

> It is in the upper part of Key Stage 2 where children who have not been supported in building their mathematical foundations quickly come unstuck.

STAFFROOM SECRET

When a child's confidence is knocked, they can label themselves as 'no good' at maths. The downward spiral then begins. If your child is struggling, it is never too late to go back to the basics. I went back to the basics in my thirties!

READ WITH YOUR CHILD

Here is a lovely one to finish on, to illustrate the progression: Georgie spent 20% of her money on a train ticket. She spent $\frac{2}{5}$ of the remainder on a meal and had £36 left. **How much money did she start with?**

Trust me, without the bar method, this is exactly the type of question that makes me spiral into fight, flight, freeze mode! However, let's calmly draw what we know and start to fill in some details. Note the shorter bar beneath the first one. This represents the remaining 80% of the money after 20% was spent on the ticket.

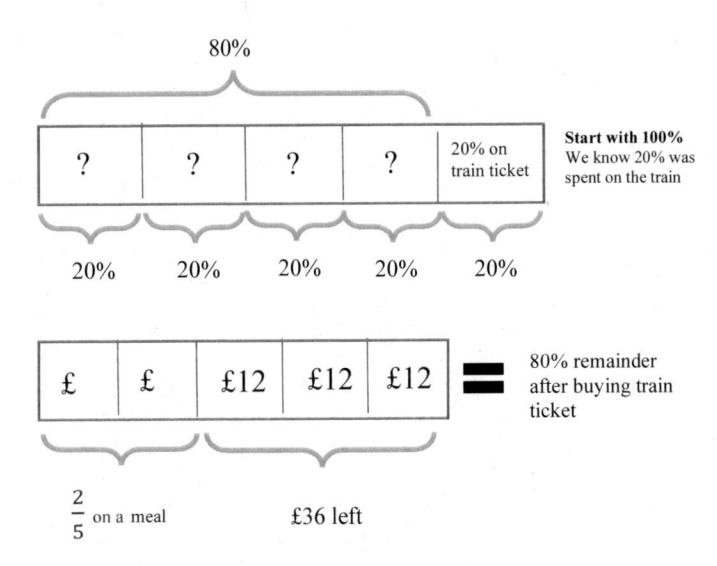

				20% on train ticket
?	?	?	?	

Start with 100%
We know 20% was spent on the train

80% above the first four cells; 20%, 20%, 20%, 20%, 20% beneath all five cells.

| £ | £ | £12 | £12 | £12 |

80% remainder after buying train ticket

$\frac{2}{5}$ on a meal   £36 left

We know **two-fifths** of her remaining money (after the train ticket was bought) was spent on a meal. We therefore know **three-fifths** must have been left to make the whole amount. We know she had £36 left, so we divide that between 3 to calculate each of the remaining **three-fifths**.

READ WITH YOUR CHILD

Breathe. If you are feeling overwhelmed, it's not unusual. You are by no means alone. Take a second look and a third… then step away if you need to. Take a break but don't give up. Always come back to it.

Now I can see what I need to calculate.

Each **fifth** has equal value, so I know the meal cost £24 as two lots of 12 equals 24. Altogether, the remaining fifths (after she buys the ticket) sum to £60.

The **total remaining £60 formed 80%** of her starting amount, as the other 20% was spent on a train ticket. I can calculate each 20% is worth **£15** by dividing **£60** by 4.

To find my **starting value**, I add each equal part together or multiply £15 by the 5 equal parts.

£15 x 5 = £75 so that is how much money Georgie started with.

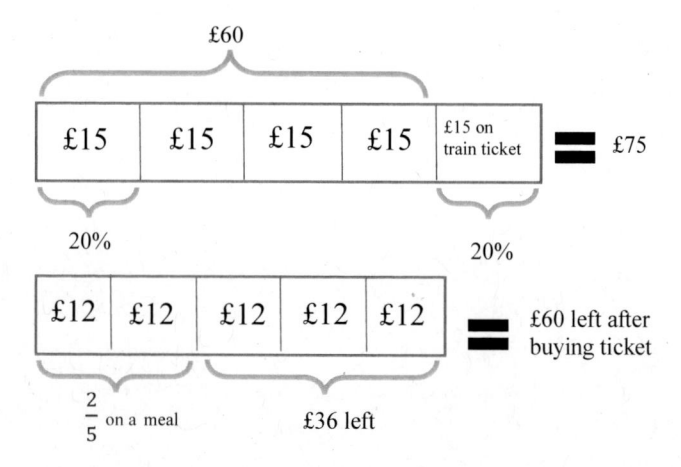

| £15 | £15 | £15 | £15 | £15 on train ticket | = £75 |

20% ... 20%

| £12 | £12 | £12 | £12 | £12 | = £60 left after buying ticket |

2/5 on a meal — £36 left

These must be practised. Start with the simple, one-step questions and work up gradually. Being aware of how word problems may be tackled in your child's classroom will enable you to support them at home. There has been a shift towards applying maths in testing; problem-solving has become a much bigger part of the curriculum. The days of completing a page of arithmetic to prove your competency are numbered!

Telling the time

It's so confusing! I mean, five minutes go by and the big hand touches the one… What does that mean? You mean to tell me when the big hand touches the two it is, in fact, ten minutes past, not two minutes past? Analogue, digital, 24-hour, o'clock, am, pm, twenty-three hundred hours, Roman numerals… What the Dickens?!

Start young! Have a clock with hands at home. Make a clock using paper-plates. When their wrist is big enough, buy them a watch. Play what's the time Mr Wolf. Talk about the time of day you do certain things at home: wake up, go to school, eat your tea, go to bed… I'd say, on average, 30 – 40% of children who start Year 5 still cannot look up at a clock and confidently tell me the time. I know it's taught, brilliantly, going through the school because I've seen it, but they forget. If they are not constantly reminded of the skill involved, they just forget, which makes negotiating 24-hour timetables and converting them into am/pm a bit of a nightmare for me, if I'm honest! When we include time zones…yikes!

When Flo was little, she liked the *Tell the Time* game by Orchard Toys. There are numerous YouTube clips available, and they are very good at breaking down what children need to know. Telling the time is a life skill which takes time to master, and parents need to invest their time in making it happen. You can't leave this to the superheroes to tackle a couple of times each year (as the curriculum allows) it needs to be practised regularly. Break it down: talk about the 'clockwise' direction the hands move in. Encourage your child to point at the clock with their finger and 'draw' clockwise circles and get them to run around in a clockwise direction. Concentrate on one hand at a time. Start with the hour hand. If you can, use a clock that you can remove the other hands from! Talk about how it's nearly 10 o'clock, or it's just gone 10 o'clock, or it's roughly halfway between 10 o'clock and 11 o'clock. Get them to focus on the hour hand and really read it without being distracted by the minutes or seconds. Montessori always said to start with the biggest picture possible and then work your way down to the finer detail. Children need opportunities to practise. Build them into your day and keep it simple. There is no rush – time is, quite literally, on your side!

Telling the time is often linked to learning Roman numerals. I use '**L**ucky **C**ows **D**rink **M**ilk' to remember the letters for 50, 100, 500, 1,000.

Time for another confession. Up until a few years ago, I was guilty of the following offence: "Honestly, what's the point? When are they ever going to need to know this stuff? A + B = C, and who cares what the highest common do-da is? The only *roots* and *pies* I need to know about are ones I put in the oven! It's a waste of their time!" Sound familiar? Firstly, from a teacher's perspective, it's not great that children hear people talk like that – it's a perfect disincentive. If that's how you feel, fair enough, but please express it away from your child's ears. Trust me, it makes life that little bit harder when children are convinced there's no credibility to what we are teaching. Secondly, there is an argument for challenging the children to come up with answers to wacky math's questions involving giraffes and scarves or insane amounts of watermelons. And although it's true, I have never used a protractor other than to teach someone how to use a protractor, I still rate the process. As an educator, I try to provide a window through which the children can experience the wider world. I can't teach them how to do jobs they haven't got yet; I'm hoping that in my room I'm teaching future engineers, designers, architects and nurses… I hope I'm teaching children who will get jobs that are yet to exist. What I can teach them, however, are key skills: problem-solving, trial and error, efficient methods, accurate measuring and recording, and perseverance. In maths, I'll challenge the children to get the answer using a different method – that could come in handy if one of the lines in their 'factory of the future' goes haywire, but they still have to fulfil an order…they'll need to find another way. By finding 'other ways', the young Sadie of the future will be more efficient and save herself time and money. Sometimes, I'll make one child teach another – not because I'm lazy, but because I need to make sure they are good communicators. When Elissa is managing her team of employees, she'll need to ensure she explains what needs to be done, clearly. When little

Alexander ends up working for a formula one team, he'll thank his lucky stars for that milestone lesson with the protractor, where he learned the importance of precision. Moreover, when I'm old and grey (greyer!) and my nurse gives me my medicine, I want it to be measured properly! So, should you find yourself about to utter words of condemnation about maths anytime soon, I'd urge you to reconsider. We all want nurse Joseph to do his job well; we never know when we'll need him.

Before we move on, I need to tell you about Jo Boaler. She is a professor of mathematics learning at Stanford University, and her principles underpin my approach to teaching maths both in the classroom and at home. Her website is *youcubed.org,* and it is full of useful resources. Please watch her short videos, which are suitable for primary-aged children because she helps children and adults to 'see' maths differently. I employed her principles in an action research project I undertook with (superhero name-drop) Mrs Huggett and Mrs Ricketts, and we were delighted and astounded by the results.

Talking of videos – I have a YouTube channel: *Staffroom Secrets* that explores the primary curriculum. The maths playlist has videos that tackle maths problems in a variety of ways – to suit different learning styles. Here, you'll see me use manipulatives, pictorial methods and abstract (traditional) techniques.

DO RE MI FA SO LA TI DO
Or should that be dough, ray, me, far, sew, la, tea, doe?

Spellings! I know how infuriating it can be because spelling is something I struggle with. I remember being lambasted about that once – something along the lines of 'that's why the education system is in such a mess'. I'd rather like to think that honest superheroes who model how to check their spelling (and are honest about their struggles) are exactly the kind of role models our children should be learning from. Superheroes remember – not superhuman.

Lottie has an uncanny ability to see a word and 'log' it. Flo is similar – there is no extraordinary effort required. Bethany learns differently – she needs the rhyme and the daily opportunity to practise: 'Look, Say, Cover, Write, Check! We used to break it down into syllables, rainbow write it (the same word over and over in the colours of the rainbow) to build muscle memory. At Montessori, we used different textures to assist the children: sandpaper letters, writing in sand, holding cut-outs of letters… You could steam up the bathroom mirror and write on that (throw in a quick chat about condensation whilst you're at it!); write in chalk on your patio, if you have one, or go to the park; type spellings on the home computer in wacky fonts; get the shaving foam out and fill up a tray before letting them loose! Spell one word by shouting it aloud to star-jumps, another whilst wriggling your bum…get physical and make it fun. If you need to be a little quieter, play hangman or get them to unravel jumbled letters to reveal their spelling. Some children get there quickly, some slowly, and others will be anywhere in-between. If you've been blessed with a learner who needs more support, you might as well get stuck in and enjoy it. It's a decision you get to make… You need to spend the time assisting the study – are you going to throw yourself all in and enjoy that time or see it as a chore and have a miserable time? The time will be spent, either way. Make sure you arm yourself with the 'spelling list' for your year group and stick it up at home. If you lose it, ask for another one and be sure to stick it firmly. Take those weekly spellings on with pride, especially if your child struggles. They will provide you with compelling evidence that having a growth mindset brings results.

READ WITH YOUR CHILD

Rhythm
Helps
Your
Two
Hips
Move

Big
Elephants
Can't
Always
Understand
Small
Elephants

Cats
On
Motorbikes
Make
It
Ten
Times
Easier
Eeeeeeeee!

The first two examples are well-known mnemonics (system for assisting the memory) to master often misspelled words: rhythm and because.

The others were made up by my class and me to master some of the words they had to remember. In some instances, they helped us with their meaning too.

In class, we spoke in ridiculously exaggerated accents: Scottish, French, Jamaican; added movements; timed ourselves for 30 seconds and wrote a tricky word down as many times as we could. We simply refused to be beaten.

The phonics rules children learn in KS1 can be incredibly helpful when learning spellings as can knowledge of prefix, suffix and root. If you do not have a copy of your school's phonic sound chart, be sure to request one.

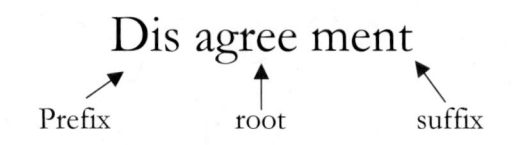

Dis agree ment

Prefix   root   suffix

When you're **forty** U shrink! FORTY
U

I always have a guilty con**science** when I forget to mark the SCIENCE books

STAFFROOM SECRET

Spelling and reading are generally tackled in school with a strong emphasis on recognising sounds (phonemes) in words. By learning phonetically, children usually build an awareness of the relationship between the sound (phoneme) and the way it is written (grapheme). The English language has about 120 different ways of writing about 44 sounds! Learning phonetically is a lot like learning to code. Blending sounds helps children to read whilst segmenting them helps with spelling. The vast majority of children in UK schools learn to read and write in this way. Some children get to grips with the 'coding' quickly – others take a little longer, and a few never really take to it at all…your school will keep their eyes peeled to see if other strategies would benefit your child. There are some lovely phonics-based activities available online: *Phonicsplay.co.uk* and good old *Twinkl* is full of phonic focused fun! Instagram and Facebook have fabulous, free content too. My one **TOP TIP:** Don't put the sound 'uh' after letter sounds! It's not F-uh, it's Fff.

Home sweet home

I wasn't really sure where to put this next bit, but here is probably as good as anywhere because it involves learning some very special spellings. Your child needs to know where they live: their address. In KS2 they'll be writing persuasive letters, and they'll need to know their address to do that authentically. I believe they should know it, as a matter of precautionary safety, as soon as possible, together with their phone number. I'd estimate 40 – 50% of the children in my Year 4 class did not know their address, and that is definitely not something the superheroes can teach them!

STOP, LOOK, LISTEN TO YOUR HEART

Are you sitting comfortably? Then I'll begin…

This is by far the most important chapter in the book. Read with your child. Read to your child. Listen to your child read. Play an audiobook and let them listen in a peaceful space. I asked a headteacher what she'd write if she were writing a book like this: 'Read with your child – I'd put that on every page.' Have you spotted it yet? Mrs Doughty, I hope you're pleased I was listening!

Every study I have seen, and every piece of anecdotal evidence I have heard, concludes children have better life chances if they read for pleasure.

Every child I have witnessed run towards their full potential is a child who reads regularly. Solid comprehension, coherent writing and a love of learning all stem from reading. Children who do not read regularly usually struggle across the curriculum.

READ WITH YOUR CHILD

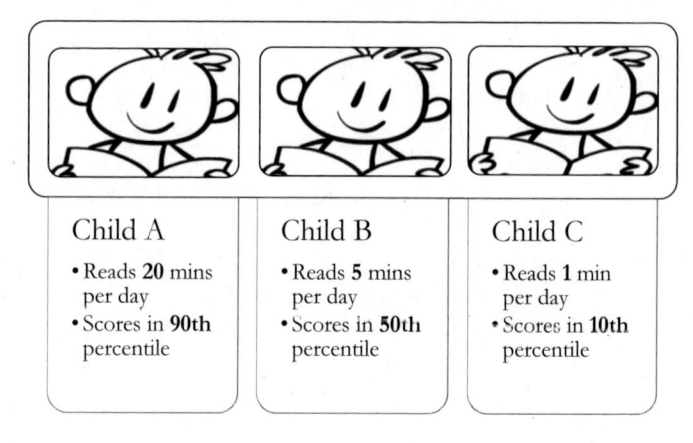

Child A
- Reads **20** mins per day
- Scores in **90th** percentile

Child B
- Reads **5** mins per day
- Scores in **50th** percentile

Child C
- Reads **1** min per day
- Scores in **10th** percentile

The data above is from a study by Nagy and Herman, conducted in 1987 and it is concerned with the correlation between reading and outcomes in standardised test scores.

Your child could read fiction or non-fiction books, magazines or newspaper (there are plenty designed for children – ask at school). If they struggle, read to them, a line at a time, and then encourage them to repeat the line you have just read. Fill your voice with meaning and encourage them to do the same.

Play I-spy: 'I-spy with my little eye a synonym for the word happy/ a proper noun beginning with the capital letter B/ a word that rhymes with jump.' TALK about what you have read. Talk about what the author is trying to do: scare you? Make you tense? Make you laugh? Puzzle you? Trick you? Make you cry? Make you turn the page? What's going to happen next? I wonder why they chose that word instead of...?

When they are writers, we encourage children to 'show not tell' e.g. 'The old man shuffled slowly, leaning on his stick; his face grimaced with each tentative step, and his pace slowed.' This sentence **implies** the old man has difficulty walking. In the sentence, the reader is shown, through descriptive language, and has to **infer** (work out) that the man has walking difficulties – they are not told explicitly. **Inference** is probably the most difficult part of comprehension.

> Authors **imply,** and readers **infer**.
>
> We ask our young readers to **infer** when they read and **imply** when they write.
>
> STAFFROOM SECRET

Comprehension skills

Unfamiliar vocabulary can usually be worked out by reading around the text and making an educated guess; predicting what is going to happen next is usually good fun, and, as long as it is based on some sort of indicators from the text, pretty much anything coherent goes! Summarising takes practice. When children first try to summarise, they typically end up lengthening the original! Sometimes they are asked to find specific passages to prove their understanding. For example: 'Find and copy the text that shows the old man finds walking difficult.' All these skills are part of reading and can be practised when you read at home, simply by chatting.

Reluctant readers

Having a reluctant reader can be frustrating; it can be heart-breaking. Parents of young, reluctant readers can worry that others are flying ahead, and their child is being left behind. Remember, in most other countries your child would not be at school yet. Try not to fall into the trap of making reading a chore to be tackled. Snuggle up and talk about the pictures: 'I wonder what they're doing here? I wonder why she's wearing that hat? Tell me about the colours you can see on this page…' Don't insist they read to you; there's so much to be gained from you reading to them. If you have them hooked, invite them to copy you – a line at a time. After a page or so, congratulate them on the effort they made, praise their strong/funny/characterful voices. Tell them how much you love sharing stories with them. Don't view reading as homework – a box that has to be ticked. Change your mindset. Remember, you're going to be spending that time with your child regardless – choose to enjoy it. Choose to cherish it. If your child has a specific need (Irlens/dyslexia/ADD, etc.) that makes reading particularly challenging, be mindful of creating the right environment in which to share your stories. Whether you read to them, you listen to a story together, or they use specific aids to help them read to you, you'll be impacting their future prospects immeasurably.

Sure, you could talk about digraphs*, trigraphs**, special friends*** and split digraphs**** but they'll be doing that at school. First and foremost, our job as parents is to

---

* Digraph – where two letters make one sound, e.g. ee
** Trigraph – where three letters make one sound, e.g. igh
*** Two or more letters that make one sound
**** Two letters, split by a consonant, that make one sound

instil a love of reading. If your child loves spotting split digraphs, by all means hunt them down, but, if you can see that makes their eyes roll, concentrate on creating the best environment for enjoying a book together.

> Reading should not be presented to children as a chore or duty. It should be offered to them as a precious gift.
>
> Kate DiCamillo

STAFFROOM SECRET

A few years ago, on World Book Day, I asked the children in my class to tell me how they felt about sharing stories at home. I wondered if (at nine/ten years old) they felt too 'big' for that, or if it embarrassed them, or if they simply preferred to read alone. I gave them some time to chat with their friends about it. Some spoke warmly, and with surprising detail, about sharing stories; sadly, many wished they could do it more often. Many said that now they were big, their parents didn't want to listen to them anymore. Some children confessed their parents hadn't shared a story with them for years. If only their families could have seen them wishing for that precious one to one time…the children did not seem big at all.

I asked some of the children to tell me more (a top phrase which I highly recommended), and they were only too pleased to share how they felt about reading at home with an adult. They spoke with sincerity and used words like content, special and loved. Dr Andrew Curran would have been delighted to see all those limbic regions light up! One child, notably, hugged herself and smiled: 'safe and snug.' Some, however, admitted that reading at home was something they did their best to avoid. Our fantastic TA Tracey Wakefield was having none of that! She set up 'Love of Reading Club' that very day, and the reluctant readers agreed to give it a go. She read. The children listened. They snuggled up, and Tracey worked her magic. It became the most hotly anticipated part of their day.

A confident reader will become a confident storyteller. 'So what?' you may ask. 'There are only so many JKs and Dahls needed! What good will storytelling do my child in the long run? They want to be an inventor/a YouTube sensation/the Wales rugby coach. Storytelling is not a life skill.' We mustn't forget that stories come in all shapes, sizes and guises. Donald Trump, love him or loathe him: storyteller extraordinaire! He can spin a yarn and hold everyone's attention. He proves that a great storyteller has great power. If you want to lead, inspire, create, change or challenge you'll need to be a great storyteller. Realities are shaped by the words we conjure; dreams are built on the affirmations we declare. The words we utter will eventually become our legacy. We need to ensure our children are equipped to create great stories, so their words can become even greater realities.

IT AIN'T OVER TIL IT'S OVER
I have put on a little weight, but I'm not singing yet!

I know opportunities are easier for some to come by than others. I know some children play polo whilst others kick cans. But I think it's important to remember that life isn't always rosy on the other-side of the street. Being a child from any walk of life can have its challenges. I now reflect on some of the most challenging times in my childhood with a surprisingly thankful smile. My childhood came with lessons on resilience built-in; overcoming challenges was part and parcel of everyday life. I learned how to barter, to think creatively, to 'get over it', and to make do. I learned to negotiate some tricky relationships with peers from diverse walks of life, and (in the shadow of my stoic mum) how to fight for what was right and just. Not all children are so lucky – my youngest two girls have missed out on many of those valuable lessons by virtue of our 'comfortable' lifestyle. I find myself trying to artificially squeeze such lessons into their lives. Beth, the eldest, had her fair share of early hurdles to overcome (bi-lateral kidney cancer will do that to a girl) and, although I obviously wouldn't wish that on anyone, she is a hardier woman for enduring her unique challenges.

I think that, on the whole, children are less resilient now, but that's not their fault, it's ours (society's). It's almost unheard of for them to play out (unsupervised) until teatime or spend all day out on their bikes, learning life's lessons. That's why there has been a rise in, for example, Forest Schools, to artificially inject some key skills and resilience back into our children's sanitised lives. Many find the challenges they face in school difficult to cope with because challenge is not part of their wider experience, and so they are ill-equipped to confidently tackle it. It's another part of the modern-day tapestry that works against our children, and we need to be acutely aware of it. Wrapping them in cotton wool numbs their senses…dare to let them be daring!

Safeguarding

Whilst thinking about the vast array of backgrounds children come from, it is important to also consider their commonality; in doing so, we highlight their shared, undeniable vulnerability. When we think of neglect or emotional abuse, we often picture families from an impoverished socio-economic background. However, research highlights that neglect in middle and higher-class affluent families is an under-reported, often hidden problem. Emotional neglect, for example a lack of quality time, and excessive pressure on children to be high achievers are factors that create psychological and emotional problems for children in adulthood.[*] Abuse can be emotional, psychological, sexual, physical or in the form of neglect. Regardless of race, class, gender, religion, ability or sexual orientation, every child is vulnerable, and we all need to have our eyes and ears open. I take safeguarding very seriously, not just as a teacher but as a parent. If you suspect any child is at risk, always talk to your school's safeguarding officer – not your mum or your friend or your neighbour – the child in question deserves the best of you, so the safeguarding officer or the NSPCC should be your first point of contact. Keep your conversations confidential; you could compromise the child's safety if you do not.

Pushing the limits

There is a fine line between pressure and support. I've seen the ill effects manifest in children whose parents push and push them to be better than others; it is a dangerous trap which ultimately damages the child and their relationship with their parents. Healthy motivation comes from within the child. Our job, as parents, is to provide the right environment for healthy self-motivation to grow. Model being a learner; model curiosity; model reading; and model struggling to solve problems with optimism and grit. Promote learning with low-pressure chit-chat, games, silly songs and stories. In my experience, most children put enough pressure on themselves – the last thing they need is for the significant adults in their lives to pile on even more. Do not compare your child with others; they are on their own journey. At parents' evening, don't ask questions like, 'Are they at the top of the class?' It sends the wrong message

---

[*] Luthar and Becker, 2002

and highlights your misplaced priorities. Besides, we can't possibly share other children's data. It's better to ask how they are progressing or if there are areas of weakness that would benefit from being explored further at home. We measure writing, speaking, listening, comprehension, spelling, arithmetic, problem-solving, shape and measure…the list goes on! The aim is for your child to reach the expected level, across the board. We base our assessments on a combination of formative (teacher assessment as we go along) and summative assessment (end of term tests). In some areas, a child might perform a little beyond the statutory expectations but fall behind in others. It's not uncommon to see a mix of the two.

STAFFROOM SECRET

> It's the superhero's job to keep you informed of where your child is in relation to the EXPECTED level, not their classmates.

Interventions

If a child starts to fall behind what is 'expected', schools implement interventions: special measures to help them catch up. They are invariably taken out of class and taught in intensive groups, often missing out on subjects like art, music and PE. In these sessions, they typically revisit what they did in the morning. In my experience, children resent being there; they want to be with their peers, enjoying something other than maths or English. By doing your bit at home, you are doing all you can to make sure your child is not in one of these groups.

Special educational needs and disabilities

Some children have SEND (special educational needs and/or disabilities) which are usually diagnosed with the help of the school. If you suspect your child has difficulties which your school has not already highlighted, never shy away from raising your concern; parents know their children best, so if you feel something is not quite right, even if you can't quite put your finger on it, tell your child's teacher. Diagnosing SEND can be very tricky, especially in primary aged children, as they all develop and mature at different rates. What could be suspected as slight developmental delay in Year 2, for example, may be diagnosed as dyslexia in Year 4. Conversely, a child may display behaviours commonly found in those with Asperger's Syndrome in Year R but be socially astute by Year 3. Most superheroes have vast experience of dealing with SEND, and all schools employ a SENDCO/Learning Support Specialist (a coordinator) to help support children and families with additional needs. Many conditions are now part of our vernacular: ADHD (attention deficit hyperactivity disorder), OCD (obsessive-compulsive disorder), ADD (attention deficit disorder), Asperger's, ASD (autistic spectrum disorder), dyslexia, dyspraxia. But others, such as ODD (oppositional defiant disorder) are less well known. It's not your responsibility to diagnose your child, neither is it the teacher's – that is a medical professional's role. However, you can work together to refer your child to get them a diagnoses and treatment. Bear in mind, there is no 'typical' ASD child or ADHD child. Every child, whether they have a specific need or not, is different and unique. It is not uncommon for a child to have overlapping traits of a combination of SEND challenges.

If your child is identified as having an additional need, you'll have the opportunity to work with the school to put in place an action plan to support them. Be mindful to ask about interventions. Ensure your child is receiving a good level of support, without feeling excluded from the afternoon's activities. If your child is diagnosed with a SEND be careful not to subconsciously limit their potential. When you know what you are dealing with, it is easier to employ strategies to overcome hurdles – ensuring your child reaches their full potential.

> Keira Knightley, Orlando Bloom, Michael Phelps, Daniel Radcliffe, Steven Spielberg and Justin Timberlake (to name a few) have negotiated their SEND hurdles spectacularly well.
>
> **STAFFROOM SECRET**

Co-curricular activities and clubs

Co-curricular activities provide our children with the opportunity to express themselves, keep fit, socialise and develop life-skills. Schools offer clubs (usually subsidised for children from low-income families) that can work alongside the curriculum to enhance your child's school experience. Again, balance here is key. Don't overload your child's life. Children need their downtime too. That said, a child with a passion for an activity outside the classroom invariable does better in the classroom. Dedication to a sport or art promotes self-discipline and instils the mindset of 'practice makes better'. A child who belongs to a club can appreciate how long it takes to improve, often by observing more accomplished peers; they learn patience and how to bounce back from failing at tasks.

Beth embraced the performing arts, in various guises, throughout school and university. Alongside studying for her law degree, she ran the musical theatre society at university; she now works in production, at the BBC. Her hobbies proved instrumental in her journey to gaining employment. Lottie loves her music; the pursuit of her passion has led to her invitation to join a few orchestras, where she is meeting contacts who may well be 'instrumental' in her future. Who knows where Flo's Lego, cornet, chess, puzzle club adventures will lead her?

School is prescriptive, but other activities represent freedom of choice – children need some control over their lives; I believe it helps balance them, which is so important for their wellbeing. I love celebrating a child's achievements outside of the classroom – a karate belt, a cheerleading trophy, a recorder grade, a Blue Peter badge, a coding certificate or meal they've prepared… Such achievements often shine a light on children who might otherwise (thanks to the limited nature of the curriculum) be in the shadows. I think it's important to remind our children that there's so much more to life than maths and English, and that we value them for so much more than what they do in the classroom Monday – Friday, in core subjects.

Setting the scene

Creating the right environment in which to learn takes time. I recall, with much pride, the first time I could genuinely leave my entire class to get on with their learning as though I were not in the room. They were self-motivated, beautiful music (Holst's, The Planets) was playing in the background, and each child was engrossed in a task of their choosing to do with the Solar System. I was simply there to watch them develop spontaneously. Montessori's words rang in my ears, 'The children are now working as if I did not exist.' I wished I could have bottled that moment. It took time to teach the children how to learn; I invested heavily in modelling learning – how to read effectively, how to summarise, where to look for information. I provided the resources and spent time investing in their curiosity – I made it fun! We'd sung, watched clips, read stories and discovered fascinating facts. I created an environment where they were hungry to discover more…that does not happen overnight. Be patient with yourself and with your children; when starting to introduce some of the suggestions in the book, don't bombard your children or overwhelm yourself. There is no rush. You have years to invest, not days: aspire to be the tortoise, not the hare.

'Play the game' by playing the games

The amount of stuff children have to know at a primary level is, arguably, ridiculous. However, they are going to be judged on the outcome of their SATs (Statutory Assessment Test), and that judgement is going to follow them into their GCSE years.

If you know the rules of the game, you might as well play it to the best of your ability; your child has to play – sitting on the subs-bench is not an option for them. I hope that within these pages you have found the tools and resources you need to make significant, meaningful changes.

- Engage with your child's learning, a little every day
- Focus on **relevant** material (as outlined in the previous chapters)
- Be mindful of using the **correct language**, in a playful way (create a positive buzz)
- Be kind to yourself and patient with your children

> Ditch the fear, embrace the time you spend with your child and choose to enjoy it. As the most influential teacher your child will ever have, read with them like it's the most important, wonderful thing in the world; it will change their lives, forever, for the better.

STAFFROOM SECRET

Finale!

Do re mi fa so la ti do – right, that's me warmed up! I'm ready to sing. I love being a superhero; I have the privilege of sharing my days with the most inspiring demographic on the planet. My job is challenging yet rewarding, just as learning should be. Of late, the challenges children face have become more significant, and for many the expectations are becoming overwhelming, such that healthy challenges have become detrimental struggles. I believe that parents who understand the nuances of the primary education system can rebalance the scales in their children's favour; they can get the most out of the system and those who work within it. As adults, we need to navigate the system to avoid the pitfalls and then concentrate on making our children's learning what it should be: child's play. With this little book on your shelf (be it virtual or otherwise) you are all set for your adventure, and I wish you all the fun, laughter, wonder and amazement there is to be had, which is gazillions and bazillions!

Now, be off with you. I've got a bedtime story to read, and Moon-Face, Silky, Saucepan Man, Mr. Watzisname, Dame Washalot and the Angry Pixie wait for no one…least of all me.

PRIMARY VOCABULARY:
A HANDY GUIDE

Please be aware that these definitions are designed for primary aged children. I've purposely tried to keep things simple. The list contains the majority of English and maths terms the children are expected to know by the end of Year 6. The list is not exhaustive.

I've jotted this down as a point of reference, so you can better understand the journey your child will be taking and support them accordingly. Please do not think you should be explicitly teaching your child all of this. That would break my heart. Your children will slowly build towards mastering these skills, every day, at school; they **must** rest at home. I do hope, however, the following vocabulary list will open your eyes to what they are expected to know, and spur you on to play a few games, as suggested in the book. Sometimes, schools hand out similar lists for SATs revision in year 6, but I feel this is too little, too late. When given out that late, the lists can create an overwhelming panic and sense of impending doom! I believe parents should have the information from the beginning of school, so they can appreciate the journey their children are on and converse with them accordingly. Playing the games in the book will support your child throughout their primary education and ease their burden; the games will help you pre-teach and revise with your child by normalising the language they are expected to understand.

READ WITH YOUR CHILD

ENGLISH

TERM	DEFINITION	EXAMPLE
Common Noun	Person, place, thing	Car, kitchen, bag
Proper noun	**SPECIFIC** person, place, thing	**H**arry **S**tyles, **P**aris, **C**oca **C**ola
Abstract noun	**Things** that don't **physically** exist	Freedom, love, happiness
Collective noun	The name for a group of something	Herd, troop, flock
Pronoun	Replaces a noun to avoid repetition	I, you, they, him, her…
Possessive pronoun	Shows ownership	His, hers, mine, etc.
Subject	The noun in a set of words that performs the verb (action)	The **dog** barked. In this example, dog is the subject
Verb	Action or state of being	**ACTION**: write, yell, skip **BEING**: was, am, were
Imperative verb	Commands	Chop, tie, open
Modal verb	The likelihood of something happening	should, might, could, will…
Subjunctive verb/mood	Formal speech for situations that are wishful, imaginary, contradictory to fact, conditional, demanding or hypothetical. Singular subjects are paired with plural verbs Often start with the word 'If'	If I **were** you… I wish it **were** July.
Adverb	Describes/modifies: **Verbs** **Adjectives** **Other adverbs** Answers the questions: HOW, WHEN, WHERE, WHY and HOW LONG	Modifying verb: **quickly** escaped Modifying adjective: **ridiculously** huge cake Modifying adverb: He sang **incredibly loudly.**
Adjective	Describes/modifies nouns	Huge, young, ramshackle
Comparative adjectives	To compare	Better, smaller, happier
Superlative adjectives	To show the most, least, best or worst	Highest, kindest, most generous

TERM	DEFINITION	EXAMPLE
Main clause	Every sentence has a '**main**' or '**independent**' clause. It's the part that would still make sense if you took all the other words away. It is a **simple** sentence.	**The cat sat on the mat.** Without a care, **the cat sat on the mat.**
Subordinate clause	These give extra information. They do not make sense without the main clause. If the subordinate clause is **BEFORE** the main clause, be sure to add a comma!	**Without making a sound**, the cat sat on the mat.
Embedded subordinate clause that uses punctuation for parenthesis	These sit within a sentence. If removed, the sentence should still make sense! Punctuation can be commas, dashes or brackets	The pirate, **who stank of grog**, fell asleep. The pirate **(**who stank of grog**)** fell asleep. The pirate **–** who stank of grog **–** fell asleep.
Relative subordinate clause	Begin with either: who, which, whose, that, where or when	She lives in Scotland, **which** is a beautiful country.
Preposition	The 'relationship' between nouns and other words in a sentence, usually involving: direction, time, place. The preposition is usually followed by a noun, which is the object of the preposition	e.g. on, before, after, towards, with, about… Nobody can arrive **before** Saturday.
Coordinating Conjunctions	Join two **main** clauses and has a **comma** before it: **F**or **A**nd **N**or **B**ut **O**r **Y**et **S**o	I think you would enjoy the bike ride**, but** I don't mind if you'd rather stay at home.
Subordinating conjunctions (the clause it is in must contain a verb)	Words that show a relationship between the subordinate and main clause. E.g. because, until, although, since	**After** she ate her meal, she burped very loudly!

TERM	DEFINITION	EXAMPLE
Active voice	The subject (dog) is active	The dog caught the ball.
Passive Voice	The subject (ball) has something done to it. I tell the children to look out for the word 'by'	The ball was caught <u>**by**</u> the dog.
Simple present tense	Without a suffix (ending)	I walk She lives He goes
Simple past tense	A completed action	I bought She sang They sailed
Present perfect tense	Started in the past but still continues	She **has lived** there for years. It **has been** raining for a long time.
Past perfect tense	Something that happened BEFORE something else	I **had danced** before becoming a teacher. She **had never been** to the zoo before last year.
Present & past Progressive	The verb to **be** with **ING**	I **am wearing** They **are watching** We **were playing** She **was swimming**
Determiners	Introduces a noun and lets us know a bit more about it!	**The** apple **An** apple **Three** apples **Many** apples **Every** apple **Those** apples
Exclamations	Always start with WHAT or HOW **But** you can use exclamation marks (the punctuation) without them.	**How** silly of him to take that! **What** a lot of things children need to know!
Antonym	Words of opposite meaning	**Hot:** cold **Quiet:** loud
Synonym	Words with a similar meaning	**Run:** sprint, dart **Walk:** amble, stroll

TERM	DEFINITION	EXAMPLE
Alliteration	Repetition of the beginning sound in words	**S**he **s**ells **s**eashells...
Onomatopoeia	A word that imitates or resembles a sound	Bang, fizz, boom
Simile	Comparing two things using like or as	As funny **as** a clown. She was **like** a wise old owl.
Metaphor	Saying something **IS** something else	Mr. Jack **is** a walking dictionary.
Personification	Giving human qualities to non-human things	The sun **smiled** down on her.
Idiom	Quirky expressions	It cost me an arm and a leg.
Hyperbole	Exaggeration	I'm starving! I couldn't sleep at all last night.
Prefix	Letters at the beginning of a root word which change its meaning	**Un**happy **Tele**vision **Mis**understand
Suffix	Letters at the end of a root word. Sometimes the spelling of the root word has to change slightly	Grow**ing** Interest**ed** Carry – carr**ied** Happy – happ**iness**
Contracted words	Two words brought together with an apostrophe	I'll (I will) They've (they have)
Compound words	Two words join to make one	Honeymoon Earring Popcorn
Hyphenated words	Hyphens are used to combine words to show their meaning is linked	Two-year-old Sapphire-blue Thirty-seven

READ WITH YOUR CHILD

MATHS

TERM	DEFINITION	EXAMPLE
Place Value	The value of each digit depending on where it sits in a number. The digit 7 in our example REPRESENTS 7 thousands	**7,236** 7=thousands 2=hundreds 3=tens 6=ones
Digit	A single symbol	The digits range from 0 - 9
Rounding	5 or more: let it soar 4 or less: let it rest Rounding can be to the nearest 1, 10, 100 etc.	Rounded to the nearest 10: 1,206 rounds to 1,210 1,304 rounds to 1,300
Estimating	An educated guess	I estimate there are 150 people in this pub
Roman numerals	Letters which represent numbers: I, V, X, L, C, D, M	1,5,10,50,100,500,1000
Inverse operation	Add is the inverse of subtract. Multiply is the inverse of divide	10x5 = 50 50÷10 = 5
Multiples	Any given number multiplied by another whole number	The fourth multiple of 5 is 20.
Common multiples	A multiple that is common with 2 or more numbers	12 is a common multiple of 4 and 6: The third multiple of 4 = 12 The second multiple of 6 = 12
Factor pairs	Pairs of numbers which multiply to produce a given number	Factor pairs of 12: 1 and 12, 2 and 6, 3 and 4.
Common factors	Factors that two or more given numbers have in common	Common factors of 12 and 16: 1, 2 and 4
Commutative law	Regardless of where numbers are placed in an equation, the answer is not changed	8 x 7 = 56 7 x 8 = 56
Prime number	They only have 2 factors: the number itself and 1 2 is the ONLY **even** prime number	17 is prime. Its factors are 1 and 17.
Composite number	All numbers that are not prime. They have more than 2 factors	9 is not prime. Its factors are: 1, 3 and 9

TERM	DEFINITION	EXAMPLE
Square number	A number multiplied by itself	$4^2 = 16$ 4 x 4 = 16
Cube number	A square number multiplied again by the original value	$4^3 = 64$ 4 x 4 = 16 16 x **4** = 64
BIDMAS	A mnemonic to remember the order in which operations should be carried out in a calculation	**B**rackets **I**ndices (squaring/cubing) **D**ivide **M**ultiply **A**dd **S**ubtract
Fraction	Part of a whole. Made up of a numerator and denominator. The denominator shows how many equal parts there are to the whole	$\frac{2}{5}$ Two out of a possible 5 equal parts
Decimal	Part of a whole. Seen in the tenths, hundredths and thousandths place value columns	0.235 2 tenths of a whole 3 hundredths of a whole 5 thousandths of a whole
Percentage	Part of a whole. Always measured out of 100	$20\% = \frac{20}{100}$ 20 out of a possible 100
Equivalents	A given value represented in different ways	50% is equivalent to $\frac{50}{100}$ which is equivalent to $\frac{1}{2}$ which is equivalent to 0.5
Quotient	The result from dividing one number by another	The quotient of $12 \div 2$ is **6**
Dividend	A number that is to be divided	**12** ÷ 2 = 6 12 is the dividend
Divisor	The number which divides another	12 ÷ **2** = 6 2 is the divisor
Improper fraction	Where the numerator is greater than the denominator, so the value is GREATER than 1 whole.	$\frac{12}{8}$

TERM	DEFINITION	EXAMPLE
Unit fraction	The numerator is always 1	For example: $\frac{1}{8}$
Mixed number	Using a whole number and a fraction to represent an amount	$1\frac{3}{8}$ is a mixed number
Ratio	Illustrates the relativity of two or more values	For every 3 apples there were 6 cherries in the bag. Ratio = 3:6
Algebra	Where letters are used to represent unknown numbers	2 + y = 5 Therefore y = 3
Equation	An illustration to show two things are equal.	$a^2 + b^2 = c^2$
Mass	Usually measured in grams, kilograms, etc. Mass and weight are different. Weight is caused by gravity, so we'd weigh less on the moon but have the same mass ☺	The mass of my sausage dog, Winston = 4.6 kg
Capacity	The amount a container can hold	The water bottle had a capacity of 1 litre
Convert units	Change between metric and imperial as well as from, for example, cm to mm.	0.75 litres = 750ml
Perimeter	Goes around the outside!	The boundary around the farmer's field was 1,000 metres long
Area	The surface measurement of a given space	The area of the field was $62,500 m^2$
Volume	The space inside an object. Calculate length x width x height to find the volume	H = 3cm W = 2cm L = 4cm V = $24 cm^2$
Analogue	Physical	Clock with hands
Digital	Made of numbers	Digital clock
2D	2 dimensional shapes have height and width but no depth	Circles, triangles and squares
3D	3 dimensional shapes have height, width and depth	Sphere, pyramid, cube
Equilateral triangle	All three sides have equal lengths. All angles are 60 degrees	

READ WITH YOUR CHILD

TERM	DEFINITION	EXAMPLE
Scalene triangle	All three sides have different lengths. All angles are different	
Isosceles triangle	Two sides are equal. Two angles are equal	
Right-angled triangle	One of the interior angles is 90 degrees	
Parallel lines	Lines that are an equal distance apart that never meet	
Perpendicular	Lines that meet or cross at a right angle	
Symmetry	Where half of something is the mirror image of the other half	
Regular polygon	A 2D closed shape made by joining 3 or more straight sides. All sides and angles are equal	
Irregular polygon	A 2D closed shape made by joining 3 or more straight sides. NOT all sides and angles are equal	
Radius	The distance from the centre to the edge of a circle	
Diameter	Running through the centre of the circle, the distance from one edge to the other	
Circumference	The distance around the edge of the circle	

READ WITH YOUR CHILD

TERM	DEFINITION	EXAMPLE
Coordinates	These are used to find the position of a point. The x axis (horizontal) and y axis (vertical) are read to plot the point. Plot position of point (1,2)	Remember: along the corridor, up the stairs!
Translation	Moving points from one place to another	
Reflection	Each point in the shape is an equal distance on the opposite side of the line of reflection	